SWANSEA
MURDERS

SWANSEA MURDERS

GEOFF BROOKES

The
History
Press

*To my mother, Eileen Brookes,
and my mother-in-law, Elaine Hoplain.
Thank you for everything, from all of us.*

First published 2013

The History Press
The Mill, Brimscombe Port
Stroud, Gloucestershire, GL5 2QG
www.thehistorypress.co.uk

British Library Cataloguing in Publication Data.
A catalogue record for this book is available from the British Library.

ISBN 978 0 7524 9307 7

Typesetting and origination by The History Press
Printed in Great Britain

CONTENTS

INTRODUCTION

Swansea was such a seething hotbed of crime that this could never be an exhaustive guide to our troubled past. Some significant cases still remain unexplored, taunting me still. It is a shame they didn't quite make it, but a selection had to be made. But just a word to the perpetrators who might think they have got away with it by thus remaining unexposed. I know who you are.

The book has been compiled entirely from contemporary sources – court records, original documents and newspapers. In this way I have been able to find a voice for our people; for as far as I know, the words I have given them to speak are their own, as reported at the time.

There are so many people I need to thank, without whom this volume would have remained a vague intention, rather than reality. My family and friends, as always, have been patient and understanding.

The willingness of friends to provide remarkable and original artwork has been very moving. You can see for yourself how good they are; thank you Charlotte Wood, Ditta Szalkai, Gill Figg and Angela Warne-Payne. To be honest I envy them their talent, though Gill's facility with anonymous letters really should be brought to the attentions of the constabulary as a matter of some urgency.

Swansea Library and Swansea Archive have been as excellent and supportive as they always are. Liverpool Registry Office dealt with my request for Andrew Duncan's death certificate professionally and efficiently. The tragic and moving conclusion to his story has never been published before, and I am humbled by the fact that, with the help of others, I have been able to find it.

The book has taken me further afield too. I received helpful support from Berkshire Archives in Reading, where I had the opportunity to look at the records from Broadmoor Hospital. The National Library in Aberystwyth is a wonderful place, and I had the enormous privilege of looking at original court documents from the eighteenth century. It was quite a thrill.

The National Archive in Kew continues to astonish me. What a wonderful place. The story of poor Kate Jackson is merely an example of all those other silent stories that lie there, waiting patiently to be revealed.

Murder? Not a nice idea. And sometimes the piling up of madness on top of cruelty and anger has been hard to deal with. But in the end this book is about the people of Swansea. I could not have written it without the strenuous efforts made by our ancestors to get drunk and attack each other, often for what in retrospect seems to be no good reason. Without their commitment to drunkenness and idiocy, this book could never have been written.

CASE ONE 1730

WHEN HEAD RULES HEART ...

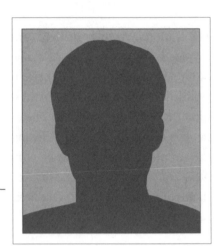

Suspect:	Nehemiah Rees
Age:	Unknown
Charge:	Manslaughter

Like so many other stories here, this started on a Saturday night in Swansea.

Why am I not surprised?

Morgan Mathews came from Cardiff and was described as County Fiddler – an unusual title, which may imply that he had some kind of obligation to entertain, an important factor in this story. He had been lodging with Roger Rosser in the town for a couple of weeks. Sadly, his musical gifts do not seem to have nurtured a serene personality; he was known to be quarrelsome and to complain all the time.

On 18 October 1730 he was out drinking in John Read's public house with a crowd of men he didn't know. But he was convivial enough. He called for ale. It was approaching midnight and everyone was both lubricated and excitable.

But when Roger Landeg asked Morgan to play the fiddle, he seems to have refused, saying that he was not working, and anyway, he hadn't got his instrument with him. Landeg got stroppy and called him a fool and a villain, and probably worse. I mean, what was the point of a County Fiddler if he was not prepared to fiddle? His stepson-in-law, Nehemiah Rees from Llangyfelach, got involved too.

A fight was brewing and so the landlady threw them out. They went into the entry, where they fought in the dark. After a while they spilled on to the street. Here Rees started banging Mathews repeatedly on the head with the handle of his whip.

Roger Landeg was mightily impressed. 'God-a-mercy Miah! Well done, Miah!' he cried. He was clearly impatient for the invention of rugby.

Soon Roger joined in, though his pals were keen to say that they had tried to stop him from doing so. Apparently family honour was at stake. And so he left Morgan Mathews with painful reminders of their family bond and traditions.

For his part Mathews, always ready to live the drama, cried out, 'I am murdered! I am murdered! Bring a light, for the Lord's sake!'

The fight was broken up. They took him to the brewhouse to wipe him down. He certainly seemed to have lost a lot of blood – his clothes were soaked through.

When he staggered back to Rosser's house the following morning he was covered in blood, with his handkerchief tied around his head, 'still concerned in liquor'. He said that Landeg had killed him, which you might

'I am murdered! I am murdered!'

think was an exaggeration since he had just walked home. Morgan took to his bed, telling Rosser that he could have fought Rees on his own, no problem, but Landeg had tipped the balance and that wasn't fair. He had been lying on top of Rees, which had exposed him to Landeg's brutal attentions. He had had a bit of a 'booting'. If he had been underneath Rees it would have been better. As it was, he was beaten all over. He complained particularly about being kicked in the heart. He had contusions to the back and the scrotum.

He went off on Monday to Mr Whitney the apothecary to have his wounds dressed. He was badly beaten, but his skull did not appear fractured. They met again on Tuesday in the market, when Mathews said he was improving, and he went to be treated again on Wednesday and Thursday.

He seemed to wander around for the rest of the week, complaining to whoever would listen. When asked by a neighbour, Jane Henry, if he forgave the perpetrators, he said he forgave their souls but wanted their bodies punished. He let everyone know that he would apply for a warrant for their arrest but that he would be ready to patch up any differences if they would give him a 'handsome treat' and say they were sorry.

Mr Whitney later observed that the wounds were healing nicely. But this was 1730, and of course they had no way of knowing what was happening within, unseen.

Morgan Mathews was right. He had been mortally wounded.

Suddenly on Saturday, a week after the assault, he contracted a violent fever. Mr Whitney was called, along with the surgeon Rowland Richard. They found him delirious, and he had lost the power of speech. He declined rapidly and died on Sunday at 2 p.m. Perhaps there was a haemorrhage of some kind; a clot; a fracture. But unless he had been beaten again on his way home that night, then it was clear who had done it.

A prosecution was brought by Anne, Morgan Mathews' wife. Rees and Landeg were arrested, though the latter died in prison whilst awaiting trial. Rees pleaded not guilty of murder but was found guilty of manslaughter. The medical evidence suggested that the wounds had contributed to Mathews' death, but they were not the direct cause. He had died of a fever of some kind. Perhaps it would have happened without him being involved in a fight. Rees, for his part, prayed benefit of clergy. This was sometimes used in manslaughter cases to mitigate a possible death sentence. Originally the condemned had to read from the Bible to indicate a level of scholarship, but since psalms could be memorised, that requirement had been dropped. The condemned would be burnt or branded on the thumb. It was an option you could only choose once. When you appeared in court, you would have to flash your thumb to show that you didn't have any previous, as they say. A bit like having points on your licence, I suppose. And no matter how painful it would have been to have been clamped down and burnt with a red-hot iron, and then in Rees' case to face six months' hard labour, it was better than the alternative.

At this point, the curtains on the life of 1730 are drawn. The threads that remain loose cannot now be tied together. Questions will forever remain unanswered. But you will see as we progress through the rest of our history, that the themes outlined here – of drunkenness and random violence – keep repeating themselves with depressing regularity.

CASE TWO 1761

AIMING HIGH

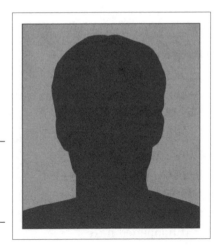

Suspect:	James Bell
Age:	Unknown
Charge:	Murder

Once again, our story starts with drinking. Young men, drinking until the early hours of the morning? Even in June 1761, it rarely went well.

These were servants to military officers stationed in Swansea. Richard Matthews, Evan Austin and Edward Goodwin were drinking with James Bell, from County Down in Ireland, who was servant to Captain Gordon. Their new friend was George Thomas, a labourer from Llangyfelach. The barmaid, Diana Watts, heard them and was later able to report what had gone on. Just as well. You do wonder how much they could remember themselves.

The servants were showing off, their military connections giving them thrilling access to firearms. Between them they had a couple of hand guns, some powder and lead shot borrowed from their masters, and obviously masses of bravado with which to impress a labourer from Llangyfelach. After all, it was three o'clock in the morning, they had been together for a while and there was nothing they couldn't do. Diana was quite clear that it was George's idea. 'Let's go out on the Burrows and do some shooting,' he said. He was keen to experience the servants' considerable prowess. So off they went, just before 4 a.m.

They started off with a piece of driftwood, to which they fastened a piece of white paper to act as a simple target, but that seemed to be a bit tame and they got bored. So Evan and James followed a bird as it swooped along the beach with their guns primed, but it wouldn't stay still long enough for them to get a decent shot.

Then James had an idea. 'Let's shoot at George's hat.'

And George said, 'That's a good idea.'

What a stupid thing to say. You wouldn't do it, would you? This was Swansea, not Switzerland, and James was no William Tell. And you just know what happened next.

I mean, be fair, he got the hat. Shot it right off. But not quite precisely enough.

James stood about 4 yards away. He held the gun in both hands, took careful aim and shot George in the head. It was a mortal wound, gouging out a fatal patch in George's skull 4in square and

(Original illustration by Charlotte Wood)

1in deep. George had the time to cry out, 'My God!' before he fell down dead. Bell dropped the gun, lifted him and cradled him whilst the others ran off for help.

As they returned, they saw James disappearing into the distance. He ran across the sands, jumped a hedge, into a garden, then a hayfield, and they lost him. The knowledge that he had hit the hat was perhaps scant consolation in such circumstances.

'It was a mortal wound'

James Bell was soon apprehended, and in court pleaded not guilty to murder, which you can understand; though he would, of course, have been bang to rights on any charge of idiocy. The charge was that it was deliberate, and they searched for a motive, for some sort of grudge, festering somewhere. But there wasn't one. It was rank stupidity. You could see it.

He had no goods nor land, nor anything to confiscate. All the authorities had was the gun, to the value of 20s. Except it wasn't even his.

James Bell was found guilty of manslaughter, and like Nehemiah Rees before him, prayed benefit of clergy. He escaped the gallows, but he too was branded on the hand.

You see, stupidity is timeless. But perhaps it does serve a purpose – as nature's way of selecting those who should contribute to the gene pool. George was simply not up to the mark. But then, was James?

CASE THREE   1805

THE PROBLEM WITH SPIRITS

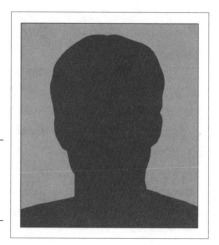

Suspect:	Morgan Williams
Age:	Unknown
Charge:	Murder

Although the records of this case are not complete, the basic facts are very simple. Morgan Williams was charged with murdering Margaret Phillips, his servant, on Saturday 19 October 1805.

Morgan returned home for his supper at 7 p.m. His servant, Margaret Phillips, who was forty but apparently looked more like forty-five, served him potatoes and butter and plonked it on a chair next to him. 'Is this all the butter?' he asked.

'It is,' she said, 'and if you want any more, you can go to the dairy and get it yourself.' Perhaps working relationships had become a little strained.

Certainly Morgan was not best pleased. But Margaret made it worse by saying that she had seen the ghost of his brother, just as some of the other servants had. Whether he had appeared to them to make an accusation about his own death, or to announce the imminent demise of another, isn't recorded. This was Swansea, not Elsinore, and Morgan was no Hamlet, but it threw him into a rage. He called her a 'screpy devil'. No one was sure what that meant, but he attacked her anyway.

He grabbed her, shook her violently, beat her, threw her to the ground, dragged her around and stamped on her. She screamed at another servant present, David Williams, to help her, but he was prevented by Morgan's son, William Morgan (yes, I know it's confusing), because she had caused much mischief in the family.

When she went quiet they lifted her into a chair. Morgan was in a 'distraction of grief'. He called her his 'dear little Peggy', kissed her repeatedly on her cheek and begged her to speak to him. They pulled a quid of tobacco from her mouth and tried to force her to drink spirits, but it made no difference. She was carried upstairs over the shoulders of William Morgan, dead.

Then they started to bury the truth of what had happened even before they had buried her. Servants were intimidated and told not to speak of it; merely to say that Margaret had had a fit.

This is what they told Catherine Edwards, who came to lay out the body. She commented on the mass of bruises on Margaret's hips, thighs, breasts and abdomen but was told that she had had a fit in a chair. She was buried on Tuesday.

However, one of the servants did speak to the constables, and an inquest was demanded. Ten days after the funeral, her body was exhumed and examined. Her bruises were immediately identified as the results of violence. They were 'not the marks of natural corruption or previous eruptive disease'. She had been beaten and as a result had died, so the coroner, Richard Griffith, did not feel it was necessary to open the body. He had all the evidence he needed.

It was at this point that Swansea physician Mr William Turton of High Street made his significant appearance in this case. He was a notable local figure, author of that fine volume *A Treatise on Hot and Cold Baths*, and a friend of Morgan Williams. In court he appeared for the defence. He particularly distinguished himself with his unshakable belief in his insight, and with his intuitive diagnosis. The fact that he had never seen the body did not inhibit him. He knew that the blood continues to circulate after death, and that any handling of the body can cause such bruising as was seen. After all, she was carried upstairs across someone's shoulders. Perhaps she had a tumour. Or a spasm. Or a rupture of an artery. Perhaps she had choked on the tobacco she was chewing, or the brandy they had given her. Since the body wasn't dissected, how could they know?

The judge, Justice Hardinge, listened patiently and told the jury to disregard his evidence. The death of Margaret was, he told them, 'a depraved and cruel outrage'. It was his view that this was clearly a case of murder.

The jury retired and returned very quickly with a verdict of guilty of manslaughter.

When he heard it the judge threw a fine strop. A man not always noted for his humanity had a huge rant at the jury. It is over 200 years ago now, but you can hear the incredulity in his voice. Manslaughter? You've got to be joking. The jury had 'abused their power and violated their duty'. Why

'a depraved and cruel outrage'

had they listened to Dr Turton? He had never even seen the body. No matter how many said that Morgan Williams was peaceable and good natured, it made no difference.

'Hundreds have been executed for murders less aggravated than yours, less depraved and cruel.'

The verdict was entirely perverse. What difference did it make whether Williams had his shoes on or not, as one witness had said? Did it hurt less? He was the reason she was dead. Without his assault on her, she would still be alive. The judge reflected that this was the second time he had been in Glamorgan and presided over a servant being ill-treated and murdered by a master (possibly a reference to the case of William

Thomas of Rhossili, who was executed for cruelty which resulted in an eight-year-old servant dying of neglect).

'God of Mercy! Are servants to be thus treated?'

But his hands were tied by the verdict. There was no longer the burning of the hand that we saw in the cases of James Bell and Nehemiah Rees. That had been superseded, though no matter how cruel that was, Hardinge half regretted its passing. But he was confident that Morgan Williams would be branded – by his conscience.

(Author's collection)

'The abhorrence of your character in every feeling heart will pollute your path and your bed.'

He had no option but to impose a fine, which the law expected to be moderate. But this was a wealthy man. So instead of the usual shilling, he imposed a fine of £50 which he described as moderate, in view of the fact that he was guilty of murder. In addition, Morgan Williams was imprisoned for a year.

Dr Turton later wrote a letter to the *Cambrian* newspaper about the trial. He commented that since Morgan Williams didn't understand a word of English, there was no point in him being in court. He may as well have stayed in his cell during the trial.

The fact that court proceedings were in English, and those involved often only spoke Welsh, would persist for most of the century. Dr Turton also reflected that throughout the trial, Justice Hardinge publicly consulted the coroner 'upon some trifling malady in one of his sides'. He should have paid more attention, but then again, Margaret was only a servant.

CASE FOUR 1832

TAKEN
AS RED

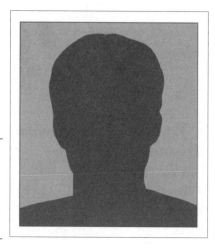

Suspect:	Robert Thomas
Age:	Unknown
Charge:	Not formally charged

There is a gravestone of Eleanor Williams in Felindre, which in any circumstances would not be regarded as remarkable. It is in the cemetery of the Nebo Independent Chapel, at the start of the steep hill that leads up towards Llwyngwenno Farm, where she lived – and beyond to Gelliwastad Common.

The words upon it have eroded and it now leans forlornly against the west wall, above the old mill.

Eleanor's gravestone leans against the cemetery wall. (Author's collection)

There is another, more famous, stone like this one in Cadoxton, in Neath: The Murder Stone, proclaiming the unsolved murder of Margaret Williams in 1828. This one dates from 1832. But the similarities are uncanny.

Two young women, both called Williams. Both country girls from Carmarthenshire, working in service. Both were killed on a Saturday night, during weekends when the winds were high.

And both were pregnant.

The wording on the stones is almost identical:

1832

To Record Murder

This stone was erected by general subscription over the

Body of Eleanor Williams aged 29 years

A native of Carmarthenshire living in service in this hamlet of Llangyfelach

With marks of violence upon her person she was found dead in a well

By Llywngwenno Farmhouse then in the occupation of Thomas

Thomas on the morning of Sunday December the 9 1832

Although

The Savage Murderer may escape for a season the detection of Man yet

Doubtless God hath set his mark upon him either for time or eternity

And

The cry of blood will assuredly pursue

him to a terrible and righteous judgement.

Such powerful words. Such desperate words. Because the murderer of Eleanor Williams was never brought to justice.

Poor Eleanor's death received little coverage. The paper was full of General Election news. There had been a shift in the affairs of the nation. How could the fate of a humble servant girl compete with this?

We are told about the great and the good; their speeches, the congratulations. The Reform Act had been introduced, and the number of Welsh parliamentary seats had increased from twenty-seven to thirty-two. This was a time of great change. The *Cambrian* stated: 'It is rumoured that a great number of disorderly persons have got into the new parliament.'

Someone far more 'disorderly' was loose in Felindre. Eleanor's life ended suddenly and horribly. On 9 December 1832 she was found dead in a well near Llwyngwenno Farmhouse.

Such a dark night. Such a long night. Such an isolated spot.

There is still something about that image that disturbs: a woman thrown into a dark hole. Was she already dead? The evidence is not clear. The report says that she had been beaten and killed, her skull fractured. Her body had on it other marks of violence. There was a 'patient investigation' by the coroner, Charles

'Such a dark night. Such a long night. Such an isolated spot.'

Collins, and the verdict reached was one of 'wilful murder against some person or persons unknown'. There were rumours surrounding the death; of course there were. It was a very small community after all, but the paper refused to speculate upon them. 'Several suspicious circumstances have however transpired, which it is not thought to be prudent to publish at present.'

Such reticence. Their belief was that every effort was made in the neighbourhood to bring the foul assassin to justice. It was surely only a matter of time before an arrest was made.

Such hope was misplaced. It was a stormy night, and there was no light of any kind. The darkness, to our contemporary eyes, would appear to be profound. There were never going to be any eyewitnesses. Evidence was never going to be anything other than circumstantial.

A collection was made to erect the gravestone and memorial. It has a poignant detail. Almost lost in the ragged, uneven grass in front of the grave, you will find a small stone, representing Eleanor's unborn child.

A community did its best, convinced that they knew who did it. But conviction isn't proof. The words at the bottom of the stone acknowledge that human endeavour had failed. They must wait for the Divine Justice that would surely come. Eventually.

And if you believe, then it brings some consolation. Under the rough grass at the bottom of the stone there is the faintest memory of the famous quotation from Romans 12:19, in Welsh (written here in English).

Beloved, never avenge yourself but leave it to the wrath of God, for it is written, Vengeance is mine, I will repay, says the Lord.

The stone speaks of vengeance and retribution. But it is an admission of failure; God's agents in this world have failed. Now it is up to Him.

We owe it to Eleanor to remember what little it is that we now know.

The winter nights were dark. They were long. And women were vulnerable.

Who had she met? Was it a chance encounter with rat catchers, whose appearance in the area so exercised the newspaper? Or was it a planned meeting with a lover? Why else would she be outside on a wild night?

And why does the stone carry two names – Eleanor, and the name of the tenant farmer Thomas Thomas? There is a reason why his name was carefully chiselled for all to see. You see, this rather small and enclosed little village was convinced that it was Robert Thomas, the son, who did it. He was the father of her unborn child, and he needed to free himself of Eleanor so that he could marry. But the locals could not forget. It is said that they painted the gates of the Nebo Chapel red on his wedding day. They painted parts of the road red too. They wouldn't leave him alone. They would not let him forget.

The tails were cut off his cows in August 1844, and, in September, one of his cows was killed. A year later he was bound over to keep the peace, his temper having got the better of him in a local dispute.

And that memorial was always there, always in his eyes.

In June 1849 he was in court again. He was described as 'a most singular character', whatever that means. He was charged with maliciously damaging the monument to Eleanor. Part of it had been knocked off and smashed into pieces. It had recently been painted.

The *Cambrian*, reporting the incident, added: 'This, it appears, is annually done by the inhabitants of the place – with red paint – in commemoration of the bloody deed.'

This particular year, this annual accusation had pushed Robert Thomas over the edge. Footprints were found in the graveyard which matched one of his shoes. A hatchet was found in his kitchen, with marks of red paint on it. He was fined 15*s* as compensation for the damage he had done, with costs of £1 8*s*.

DESTROYING THE MONUMENT ERECTED AT VELINDRE CHAPEL YARD, TO THE MEMORY OF ELEANOR WILLIAMS, WHO WAS BASELY MURDERED IN 1832, IN THAT NEIGHBOURHOOD.—*Robt. Thomas,* of Llwyngweno, farmer, a most singular character, was summoned to answer a charge of maliciously damaging the above monument, which charge was clearly brought home by the following circumstantial evidence :—P. S. Price deposed that on Saturday the 12th of May last, I visited the yard of a Dissenting Meeting-house, at Velindre, in the parish of Llangafelach, in which yard a monument had been erected to the memory of one Eleanor Williams, who had been murdered, near Velindre, in 1832. I found that the

From the *Cambrian* Newspaper. (By kind permission of SWW Media)

But he could neither erase the memories of others, nor destroy the gravestone. It is still there.

It seems so degraded, lost and mossed in the corner of a chapel graveyard. And now, as Eleanor's headstone gradually crumbles and fades in the weather, she is consigned to be slowly forgotten by history, just as Robert Thomas wanted.

CASE FIVE 1845

SUCH A STRAIN

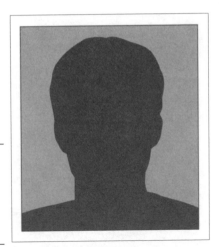

Suspect:	George Beynon Gibbs
Age:	Twenty-four
Charge:	No charge

George Gibbs, fifty-eight, a farmer from Overton, Port Eynon, died in suspicious circumstances in May 1845.

A troubling story started to emerge at the inquest when his daughter Elizabeth spoke, and appeared 'considerably affected in giving her evidence'. She described considerable tensions between her late father and her brother, George Beynon Gibbs, who had allegedly been on bad terms for some time. They had quarrelled frequently, though not in the few days preceding his death. They never ate together. George and his two daughters Eliza and Mary ate at one table, and George the Younger at another – and at different times. This is how George had breakfast on the morning he became ill. Interestingly, he had what we might call the Full Port Eynon – a bit of yesterday's lobster, three oysters and a pint and a half of beer. They have always done things a bit differently down there.

Elizabeth was certain there was no poison in the house. Certainly no corrosive sublimate, for example, which was used as a wash for sheep. She was also quite sure that no one had visited a druggist recently. Notwithstanding such exemplary domestic practices, George died painfully, exhibiting all the signs of poisoning.

The funeral was arranged, but as he was leaving for the churchyard, the arrangements were interrupted and George's coffin was reopened to facilitate a post-mortem.

It was performed by George Perry, a surgeon from Reynoldston, and George Wiglesworth, a surgeon from London visiting Swansea. The details

Port Eynon. (Author's collection)

were reported in considerable detail in the *Cambrian* newspaper, 'since it may be interesting to our medical and chemical readers'. Of whom there would be many, obviously. They noted severe inflammation of poor George's insides, and that his small intestine was perforated. Such a violent and destructive inflammation of the stomach could only have one cause – an irritant poison. So they removed the stomach, the intestines and all the fluid in the abdominal cavity and put them in three bladders. These were put in a tin case and its lid was soldered down. Off it went to Bristol, to Mr Herepath the chemist.

Upon receipt, he had a good poke around in the bladders. He found mercury, and was convinced it had been administered as bichloride of mercury – otherwise known as corrosive sublimate.

The inquest jury could only deal in facts, and not opinions, and so could only return an open verdict: George had died of an 'inflammation of the stomach and the intestines'. However, they could not speculate about how it had happened. That was for magistrates to explore.

The family dispute hung over the case like a cloud. As is often the case, the argument between father and son was about money. George Gibbs had given over his farm to his children, in return for an annuity or pension. The son wanted to sell off some of the farm stock, but George felt that this would impact on his annuity and would not agree. The younger

'a violent and destructive inflammation of the stomach'

George, who was twenty-four, had a record of violence, having appeared frequently before the magistrates. He had threatened his father. In fact, just before his death, George Gibbs had told his neighbour that his son had frequently threatened to kill him. On one occasion he had hidden from him under the bed.

The public-spirited *Cambrian* urged all local druggists to check their records to see if they had sold any corrosive sublimate recently. In fact, George Beynon Gibbs was taken by a policeman to Swansea and 'there made an object of public gaze', as he was paraded around all the chemists to see if anyone recognised him. They didn't.

At this point events took an unusual turn, one which emphasises clearly the differences between those days and our own, for the case was played out in the columns of the *Cambrian* newspaper. While the reporter was convinced 'by the serious character of the offence which had unquestionably been committed', the Rector for Port Eynon, Samuel Phillips of Fairyhill, leapt to the defence of the younger George by writing a long letter to the press. He did acknowledge that the young man 'having been in bed at so late an hour as eight o'clock, while the other members of the family were at breakfast is, I admit, a suspicious circumstance'. But he had been loading a coasting vessel with limestone until 2 a.m., so perhaps he deserved a lie-in. But he did get up when called and he did share breakfast, which were hardly the actions of a man who had laced the food with poison. The whole case, as far as Samuel was concerned, was based upon 'anonymous accusations presented to the coroner'. This had prompted the post-mortem. As a result, 'the chambers of the dead had been invaded'.

He claimed that the medicines George had taken had reacted with the vinegar he had had on his lobster, and replicated the signs of poisoning. It was thus the doctor who had done it. George was, according to him, 'a man whose constitution had been shattered by former intemperate habits – he had been subject for years to violent spasmodic attacks in the stomach, and his bowels were in a constipated state for three or four days previous to his death'.

The medical response was scathing. There could be no connection with food or medication. He had been given calomel, rhubarb, magnesia; he was bled twice and was given an enema. None of this could explain the presence of mercury in the tissues. His death wasn't normal and the question of how the poison was administered remained. Was he given it? Or did he take it himself? They had a duty to explore the details of the case.

The debate in the press, which went on for over a month, effectively ended any hope of the case being explored properly. Opinion was firmly entrenched in the public mind – and it was polarised. And George Gibbs was put in a coffin once again.

Without evidence it was impossible to pursue any accusation. George died through the 'visitation of God', simply because there was no other verdict that could be supported. The family resumed their lives. Eliza Gibbs married George Williams in 1846 and moved to Swansea. George Beynon Gibbs inherited the farm and married Mary Bevan in 1848.

Who knows what happened? Did George treat himself too enthusiastically, in an attempt to resolve a blockage? Or was he a blockage to wealth and happiness that others wished to remove? I don't know. But I do know that the perfect crime remains one in which there is no recognition that there ever was a crime in the first place.

A similar incident had been reported in Loughor in 1779, when Margaret Matthews appeared to poison her father, John Bevan. He was about to marry his servant-maid, and as a wedding gift he was going to give her a piece of land. Margaret was less than impressed, so she invited her dad and her prospective stepmother over to supper. She made some milk and flour diet, and put plenty of butter and sugar into his dish. It might sound like a blancmange, but it wasn't like anything served at a children's party. John ate it, became violently ill and was taken home. He retched, and was 'purging blood most violently' until he died at 2 a.m., declaring to the last that it was the supper that had done for him.

As you might have guessed, his stomach, when opened, was full of arsenic. Margaret may have been the mother of three children and 'of unblemished character', but the finger of suspicion pointed firmly at her. After all, hell hath no fury like a woman who can see her inheritance slipping through her fingers and into the arms of a woman who was once her inferior. But just as in Port Eynon, there was insufficient evidence. Margaret was found not guilty.

CASE SIX 1850

'HOW THINGS DO PROSPER'

Suspect:	Anne Owens
Age:	Twenty-nine
Charge:	Concealment

Stories about children are always the most moving; they are always the hardest to write about. This one is no exception.

A young boy of eleven, John Ace, was sent down to Swansea beach at St Helens to collect sand for his father. He was digging at the very top of the beach, near the 'finger post' pointing towards the Mumbles. He uncovered rags and then the foot of a child. John ran home with the basket of sand to his father, and told him what he had seen. His father went immediately to the police and together they all returned to the beach, where they immediately found the bodies of two newborn children, a boy and a girl, partially wrapped in rags. The bodies were taken the short distance to Swansea Infirmary, where they were examined by Mr Hall.

The boy was 'a very fine child and had all the appearance of having been born alive', though the girl, who was much smaller, probably was not. They were definitely twins. He felt that death had occurred due to the umbilical

'the bodies of two newborn children'

cord not being tied when it was cut, if indeed it was. But the boy had not been suffocated in the sand. It was his opinion that he had been dead by the time of his burial.

It didn't take the police too long to discover the identity of 'the unnatural mother'. It was twenty-nine-year-old Anne Owens from Horton in Gower who had, until very recently, been lodging in Orange Street with Mrs Sims, an old widow who slept with her in the same room. She hadn't realised that Anne was pregnant; she just seemed unwell with a cold. It was only after the police turned up at her house looking for Anne that Mrs Sims noticed any staining on the bed. She did, however, recall a curious incident that had occurred a few days earlier. She had gone outside to search through the ash pit for scraps of coal for the fire, and she had found a large clot of blood. When she was called out to see it, Anne looked at the lilac tree above her and said, softly, 'How things do prosper.' She then went back inside, muttering about not caring whether she went over the pier head or to the workhouse. This unsettled Mrs Sims, though she didn't know why.

Anne had previously lodged in Back Lane, where residents like Mrs Trosk were convinced that she was pregnant, though she had always denied it. Then recently, when Mrs Trosk had seen her again, Anne seemed suddenly delicate and as if she had lost weight.

When she was confronted in her father's house in Horton, Anne admitted delivering the two babies on the beach, all alone. No one else was involved. She couldn't say whether they had been born alive or dead, but she was certain that they were dead when she wrapped them and buried them where they were born. The case rested entirely upon whether the boy had been born alive, and if so, 'did the child die from natural causes or from any unfair means'. And of course there was no way of proving what had happened in the dark on the sand, when a frightened young woman let nature take its course.

Anne was found guilty of concealing the birth of the twins and was sentenced to one year's imprisonment with hard labour.

(Original illustration by Ditta Szalkai)

But the historical record contains one final and astonishing twist; one that I least expected. Because, during the trial in July 1850, the Governor of Swansea Gaol, Mr Cox, was called as a witness. He told the court that he knew Anne. He remembered her very well. How could he forget? She had done this before, ten years previously.

When she was nineteen, she was a servant at Cilibion in Gower. In January 1840 she had given birth to another boy. She had buried him in a garden in Llanrhidian.

At the time, the judge had commented that the offence of concealment would normally warrant a sentence of two years' imprisonment, but he was disposed to pass a milder sentence 'in the hope that you will take care of yourself for the future'.

She was sentenced to one year's imprisonment with hard labour.

There are so many ways in which history can repeat itself.

CASE SEVEN 1852

GATHERING LIMPETS

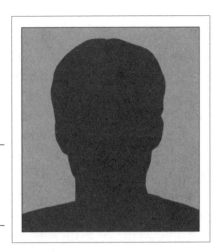

Suspect:	Mary Mahony
Age:	Around thirty
Charge:	Wilful murder

It was Saturday 10 April 1852 on High Street in Swansea. Early in the morning – at about 6 a.m. – Mary Mahony was outside the house of William Michael, the surgeon. She was found staggering about, unwell and obviously in labour. Mary was described as 'a rather tall Irish vagrant of about thirty'. She said she had just arrived in Swansea from Cardiff; looking, she said, for her husband, though not everyone believed that part of her story. She was found by Maria Rooney of Greenhill, who took her first to the police. The overseer from the workhouse came to see her, but it was obvious what her problem was. She was taken to Anorah Cochrane's house in Morris Lane. Anorah was a widow, and was asked to take her in for a small fee. There, Maria and Anorah assisted in the delivery of a healthy male child at 9.30 a.m.

Mary had no clothes for the child. She said that events had rather over-taken her, and so she hadn't brought any with her. Local people donated what they could. The clothes might have been past their best, but they were serviceable. The bed gown had holes under the arm and the shirt had a patch on it, but as Mary would later find, these clothes were easily recognisable.

She stayed in Morris Street for a week. Then on Saturday 17 April at 6 a.m. she left with the child, saying she was off to look for her husband – claiming this time that he was in Neath. She had no shoes. Anorah was concerned: she didn't think that she was fit to be out. Mary had shown herself to be a tender and kind mother. She appeared to 'nurse her baby as tenderly as any mother ought to do'. But she hadn't rested for long enough.

As Anorah pointed out, 'women immediately after confinement were liable to derangement of the head, if suddenly surprised or frightened'.

Nonetheless she left, with a baby in one arm and a bundle in the other.

Later that day she was seen again by Maria in Greenhill, with the bundle but without the baby. Maria questioned her.

'My child is out in the country, nursing with some of my friends.'

Maria did not believe her and grabbed her. 'Have you been in the country killing your child?'

A chilling idea, but not uncommon in areas of abject poverty, like the top end of High Street. Initially Mary denied it, but Maria would not let her go and dragged her off to the surgeon, William Michael, who took her to the police station. There Mary finally confessed that the child was dead. It had died in her arms and she had buried it in a hole in the ground 'in a field far away', but she couldn't remember where. Later she suggested that it was next to the railway line, on the road to Cardiff.

She emptied her bundle. She had some child's clothing, 2s 1d, a 4lb loaf of bread, some tea and sugar, and about thirty-six limpets. Generally speaking, limpets are not usually collected in the countryside. She maintained her story, even though she was covered in sand.

That morning, down in Mumbles, two friends – Herbert Evans and Thomas Jenkins, who lodged at the Angel Inn – were taking a stroll in Bracelet Bay and looked inside a small cave in the rocks at beach level. On a rocky shelf about 7ft from the ground, they saw a bundle of linen. They thought at first that it might be tools left there by workmen. The shelf was below the watermark of the average tide. Herbert poked the bundle with his walking stick, and felt some resistance. They noticed that it was a collection of baby clothes, so they fetched the police and the coastguard. They took the bundle down. The linen was a bed gown with holes under the arms, and a shirt with a patch and cap.

It contained the body of a dead male child.

There was a bruise on the left side of the child's head and his lips were blue. Perhaps the most chilling detail is that no one could have placed the poor child there. It would have had to have been thrown up on to the ledge.

The cold body of the child was examined by the inquest jury in the Mermaid Inn in Mumbles. He was seven days old and had been dead for a few hours only. Slight bruising around the mouth was noted. William Michael, who perhaps Mary had been trying to find the previous week and who had taken her to the police with Maria, had opened 'all the cavities of the body', and his conclusion was that the child had been asphyxiated. How could this have happened? By pressure from the hand? Or by being held too

'his lips were blue'

closely? Clearly this was the central question: Was it accidental or deliberate? And in his opinion it could not have happened from natural causes: 'I never examined the body of a more healthy or well-formed child.'

John Knight, an oyster agent in Mumbles, had seen a woman coming along the beach from Swansea on Saturday morning. She was wearing a patched brown dress, shawl and a white cap with no shoes, carrying a bundle and heading towards Bracelet Bay. He had taken careful notice of her in case she was about to steal his oysters.

Maria Rooney gave evidence to say that the baby was alive and thriving on the evening of Friday 16 April 1852. It was 'a strong hearty child from its birth'. No one believed that the death was accidental.

The jury thus returned a verdict of wilful murder. Mary appeared indifferent to the verdict, and was described as being in a weak state. She was taken to Swansea Gaol to await her trial at the Assizes in Cardiff.

There was only one suspect and the *Cambrian* newspaper was quick to pass sentence. It was 'the murder of an infant by its mother ... a foul and unnatural deed, of rare occurrence in the Principality'.

They ought to have read their own newspaper more carefully. Sadly it wasn't that unusual at all.

In court in Cardiff Mary was treated with more sympathy. Post-natal depression was recognised, if not defined. Perhaps that is why the details of her initial story were contradictory. She was distressed at the death of the child and became confused. The grass came down close to the cave where the baby was found. Perhaps that is what she meant by a hole in the ground. Maria Rooney had found her on the road that headed out of Swansea – perhaps she was on her way to find her husband, dejected by bereavement.

But as everyone in court realised – counsel, judge and jury – no one could say with any certainty what had happened. The slightest pressure could have caused death. It didn't have to be deliberate. The baby could have been wrapped too tightly and suffocated in a moment. There was no evidence at all that the child had been murdered. As the defence counsel said, if she had committed murder, would she have then gathered limpets? And abandoning the body? Merely the desperate action of a distressed woman.

There was only one possible verdict. Mary was found not guilty of murder and released.

In one of those horrible coincidences, the name of Mary Mahoney reappears in the historical record, this time in 1876 and in Cardiff. This Mary Mahoney was a young girl of eighteen. She was a homeless, illiterate orphan who was tried for the murder of her newborn child. She had been abandoned by the father, a soldier. She had killed the child by hitting it with a pickaxe used for breaking coal, and had tried to hide the body in a coal heap. She was sentenced to death, though she was clearly unstable. Her mood swung wildly between anguish and periods of euphoria, when she would be singing and dancing round her cell. Shortly before her execution, the Home Secretary commuted the sentence to one of penal servitude.

CASE EIGHT   1858

'A RECKLESS RACE, DISREGARDFUL OF HUMAN LIFE'

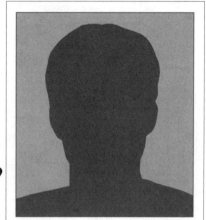

Suspects: Manoeli Selapatane
and Panaotis Alepis

Ages: Unknown

Charge: Murder

His name was Atanasio Mitropani and they found him in the canal at 9 p.m. on a cold Tuesday night, 16 February 1858. He was twenty-five, and it wasn't easy to pull him out. He was stout and well developed. And he was dead.

He was the cook on board *The Penelope*, which was loading coal. He had served on the ship for about four months, and they had been in Swansea for a few days.

It was a very busy Tuesday night. The Greek Lent celebrations were in full swing and everyone was having a good time, fuelled of course by drink. At about 9 p.m., two men, Henwood and Johns, who were working alongside the canal, heard a struggle in the darkness. They heard men quarrelling in a foreign language and fighting opposite the Ship and Castle on the Strand, next to one of the coal wharfs. There was a loud splash as someone seemed to have fallen in the water. They saw a body in the canal, which they pulled out with a boat hook. It was Mitropani.

Nearby they found a stone, a walking stick, his purse and also the bowl of a tobacco pipe. There was blood everywhere. Mitropani's head was 'dreadfully smashed'. His wounds were hideous and were still oozing. There were many deep stab wounds. His left temple was beaten almost into a jelly.

(The author's collection)

This gruesome detail is perhaps not surprising when you consider that one of the murder weapons, which was recovered from the canal side, was a ball of iron, about 2lb in weight, bound with cord and rope to form a lethal sling shot with which he had been beaten. He had a 6in fracture to the skull.

The doctor who examined the body was certain that Mitropani had been attacked by two men simultaneously. He had been stabbed from

'His left temple was beaten almost into a jelly'

the back and beaten from the front. He was already dead when he went into the canal.

Two other Greek sailors were immediately accused: Manoeli Selapatane, twenty-eight (who was actually Turkish), and Panaotis Alepis, a twenty-three year old from Sparta. They had arrived in Swansea looking for a ship on the previous Friday. They were detained within the hour at the Jolly Tar, their lodging house on Wind Street. Their rooms were searched.

Money and a key that might have belonged to Mitropani were found. The landlady, Elizabeth Lovelace, said the accused had returned a little after 9 p.m. One of them had gone straight out to the back of the house to wash a pocket handkerchief. Then he put it to dry in front of the fire. She noticed spots on it that she believed were bloodstains.

Both denied any involvement – but their protestations were ignored. There was a chilling inevitability about the case. Once they were in custody no one bothered much with any further enquiries.

The *Cambrian* newspaper condemned them immediately. After the arrest and before the trial the paper identified all Greeks as 'sudden and quick in quarrel, and addicted to the use of the knife'. It was also said that violence might be the price the town must pay for economic success, but many foreign sailors were 'hardly more than half-civilised'. Dangerous weapons should stay on board ship, since knifing people was not the Welsh way (though even a cursory examination of this book might suggest that this was self-deception).

All the details of the murder were examined carefully in court, but when you look at the proceedings today it is clear that it was not much more than a formality. It had already been decided that Selapatane and Alepis had done it. They were described in the press as 'ferocious-looking Greeks'. Their demeanour in court was too casual and was judged to be cold-blooded and contemptuous. They showed 'indifference and levity', adding weight to the theory that Spartans like Alepis 'have always been a reckless race, disregardful of human life'.

All that was required was the verdict.

As men with a shared language in a strange town, it isn't surprising that they were perhaps drawn together. Alepis and Selapatane had visited Mitropani on *The Penelope* perhaps in search of employment.

Alepis. (By kind permission of SWW Media)

Lazarus Stena, the fourteen-year-old steward on *The Penelope*, remembered seeing Alepis on the ship at about 6 p.m.

on Tuesday. Alepis talked to Mitropani, who left the ship before him, for a while. Mitropani asked Stena for a biscuit and promised to return with two apples for him. Stena confirmed that he certainly had Turkish sovereigns in his purse when he left.

Elizabeth Phillips was what the newspaper sometimes described as 'a nymph of the pavement' and her evidence was an important part of the narrative that was constructed. She had seen Mitropani quite frequently in the Powell Arms over the previous few days. In fact he had given her a sovereign on the previous Sunday in anticipation of personal services, but Lizzie had taken the money and not obliged in any way. This may or may not have been significant. She had seen him again on Monday when she thought he was in the company of the two accused, but she couldn't be sure. Then on Tuesday, between 5 p.m. and 6 p.m., she had seen Selapatane and Alepis in High Street. She took them into the Red Lion and bought them a drink, since they said they had no money. Much was made of this in court, since they had cash when arrested. But then if someone else was buying, why should they put their hands in their pockets? Selapatane warned Elizabeth that Mitropani would be coming in disguise to find her, since he wanted his money back. He offered to protect her and allegedly said: 'You are a bloody little fool that you do not put him to bed and take all his money – he is no countryman of mine.'

This was interpreted as a sign that Selapatane was trying to create a false identity. But Selapatane was Turkish. Mitropani was Greek. It might not have mattered much to the *Cambrian*, but it was a significant distinction to them.

In court, Selapatane denied ever having met Elizabeth.

The three Greeks were then seen together in a dancing house at the Powell Arms in High Street. One was wearing a scotch cap, and an identical one was found at the scene of the murder. George Jafalia of *The Penelope* identified it and said that Selapatane left wearing it at about 9 p.m.

Elizabeth Phillips and her friend Lizzie Thomas saw Alepis and Mitropani together at the station at 8.30 p.m. They knew the time because they looked at the station clock. After that they never saw them again. Someone else saw them at 8.30 p.m. at a waxworks exhibition on High Street, where Mitropani was laughed at for wearing a sheepskin coat.

Other professional girls claimed to have seen them. Mary Ann Williams spotted them near the Ivorites Arms; Frances Edwards saw them running on the Strand by the side of the canal. Sarah Lovelace saw them too, and her friend Maria Phelps recognised them as two Frenchmen. There were lots of sightings of men who looked like them, but none of it was conclusive. All of these ladies had appeared many times in court themselves, for offences like robbing sailors and throwing stones. And whilst this in no way suggests that they were dishonest in the witness box, their many convictions for being drunk and disorderly might suggest that they were not always completely reliable.

Alepis said he never spent any time with Selapatane. He had gone to the Powell Arms with someone else. Mitropani had asked him on Monday if he spoke English, because he was looking for a girl who had stolen a sovereign from him. Alepis couldn't help him, and apart from their conversation on *The Penelope* on Tuesday he had never spoken to him again.

There were no witnesses who saw them at the site of the murder. No one had seen them with weapons of any kind.

Their motive? They knew Mitropani had money; they had seen his sovereigns. Selapatane had used a sovereign to buy four two-penny mince pies from Price the Bakers on College Street. The assumption was that it was a brutal robbery. But whilst much was made of the fact that Selapatane had a Turkish sovereign, that could hardly be a surprise, given his nationality. There could be no reason to assume that he had stolen it.

The whole case against them was circumstantial and hollow. Not only that, an unexpected story emerged when Captain Feline of *The Penelope* appeared as a witness. Yes, he had given Mitropani 'two sovereigns

Selapatane. (By kind permission of SWW Media)

39

of Turkish money', the ones that Lazarus Stena had
seen. He also said that everything on board had been
amicable, with no ill will or anything, apart from the
fact that Mitropani had taken out a summons against
the second master on board, who happened to be the
captain's brother. This significant detail was margin-
alised, but deserved greater investigation.

Whilst Selapatane and Alepis had no clear
motive, there may have been others on board
with whom Mitropani had quarrelled who had
more cause. He had also been busy around
the various entertainment centres in Swansea.
Perhaps he had upset someone. Defence Counsels
Allen and Rees outlined all the inadequacies clearly.
There was no reliable identification of the two men.
No one had any clear idea of the time. It was all a matter of guesswork
amongst people who didn't have a watch and so the true sequence of
events could never be established with any certainty. If there was blood
on the handkerchief, then whose was it? Alepis said that he had had a
nosebleed, and indeed suffered from one during the trial. Neither of the
accused had ever been seen in possession of a knife.

But it didn't seem to matter much. The jury retired for twenty-six
minutes and returned a verdict of murder. They were sentenced to death.

When you look at it now, there are assumptions and inconsistencies
throughout which were never explored. But why should they have
been? Not when everyone wanted to believe that the case was solved.
A miscarriage of justice? Who can say? But it could all be wrapped up,
and everyone could move on. But no one can say for certain who killed
Mitropani. We can though say with absolute certainty how Alepis and
Selapatane died.

Awaiting execution they were visited by Revd Morphinos, an
Archimandrite of the Greek Church. As they prayed together, the horror
of their position began to slowly dawn on them. But at no point did they
confess or admit their guilt. They maintained their innocence until the
end.

They were hanged together on 20 March 1858, a few short weeks after Mitropani's death. The executions were staged in public and thousands gathered. There were showmen, and gamblers all gathered to make a small profit on the occasion of a cruel death. The Greek seamen were executed by William Calcraft, the public executioner, who used the short drop method. Their necks were not broken; the condemned were publicly and slowly strangled.

The traps were sprung at 8 a.m. Alepis died almost immediately whilst Selapatane struggled for about seven minutes. Then the crowd slowly dispersed.

Savage murder, execution, job done. Let's move on. Except it was horribly wrong.

And the captain and his brother sailed away.

CASE NINE   1865

'DIO VI BENEDICA, COME MI BENEDICE ORA A ME!'

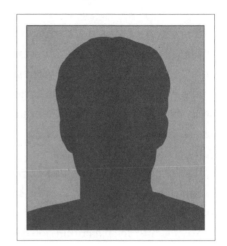

Suspect:	Francisco Giardinieri
Age:	Unknown
Charge:	Murder

There was some dispute about the victim. Everyone agreed that his name was Peter Moitch, but there was no consensus about where he came from. He was variously described as a Latvian from Riga, a Russian, a German, or a Finlander. But there was no doubt at all that in February 1865, he was lying dead in a Swansea street with his bowels protruding through a knife wound, stabbed apparently by an Italian. The only issue was, which particular Italian did it?

Peter Moitch was about thirty years old, and he had been in Swansea for about three weeks. His ship, *The Hastings*, which he had joined in Cape Town, was being repaired in dry dock. During this time he stayed at Walstrom's Boarding House in Fisher Street. He was regarded as 'a peaceable and well-conducted man'. He had stayed there before, and was known as a quiet man who never quarrelled with anyone.

On a cold Wednesday night in February he went out for the evening. At that time he was completely sober. He was seen in The Star by Stephen Bartlett, a ship's carpenter who was drinking there. It was regarded as a 'low public house' in Cross Street, but it was popular with sailors. Just before 11 p.m., about eight Italian sailors came in and ordered a quart of ale.

They sat around drinking and singing. Clearly it was a jolly evening down at The Star. You may notice that there are many stories here which are a consequence of a convivial night out amongst Swansea's finest. This is no different. Peter was perhaps a little worse for drink but he was in a jolly mood. Mary Ashton was there and Peter had grabbed her round the waist.

'his bowels protruding through a knife wound'

'Let me go, Peter,' she said.

'You don't like me, you like the Swansea chaps,' he replied. So everything was fine. There was no aggression, no quarrelling. Just teasing and singing.

And then, as the Italians were leaving, Peter Moitch struck Francisco Giardinieri's hat. It was clearly done in play. Nothing was said. But ten minutes later, Peter was lying on the ground bleeding to death.

John Walstrom was going to bed, when he heard groans in the street below. He went down and Peter was brought inside and placed on the kitchen table, but he died soon afterwards.

Almost immediately afterwards, two Italian seamen were charged on suspicion of involvement in his death. Minunzo Casettari was picked up in Walstrom's when he eventually made it home at 2 a.m. Francisco Giardinieri was arrested on his ship *Tritone*.

A knife was found by Anorah McCarthy. She was twelve years old, and she had been sent to the sawmills for sticks for the fire at 8 a.m. After finding a knife on the ground opposite Mrs Michael's furniture shop, she gave it to her brother Timothy, who used it to cut up an apple. When they heard about the murder they took it to the police.

Dealing with foreigners was always exasperating, given the language barrier, and for some people the police appeared to be less assiduous than they should have been in gathering the evidence. As we have seen with Mitropani, there was an eagerness to close the case quickly.

The inquest jury were given a picture of the murder as a straightforward crime. A German seaman, William Anderson, had seen the Italians hold on to Peter Moitch, one on each side, as they staggered away from The Star. He identified Giardinieri. They seemed to be walking quite affably arm in arm. Then outside Walstrom's, Giardinieri appeared to strike Peter. He cried out 'Oh God!', walked a couple of steps, and then fell down. Two men ran away. Anderson saw only one blow, delivered, he said, by Giardinieri with both hands together. He didn't see a knife. The man on the other side of Peter disappeared.

Another German seaman said he heard one of the Italians ask Peter if he wanted to fight; he said yes. No one else appeared to hear this.

The problem was that everyone involved was drunk, to a greater or lesser extent. Their memories and their witness statements were full of inaccuracies and inconsistencies. None of them could actually agree on much at all. There was no obvious motive, which fuelled a belief that foreigners were random killers.

Interestingly, the post-mortem revealed two stab wounds; one in the belly and a second in the small of the back. It couldn't be explained. It was an unexpected anomaly, but one which did not materially affect the case so they ignored it.

Giardinieri was found guilty, and sent to face trial at the Assizes in Cardiff. Casettari was released.

In the interim, the *Cambrian* had a chance to rage against knife crime.

The use of so deadly a weapon as the knife cannot be too strongly condemned or scarcely too severely punished. It is a cowardly and unmanly act and whatever complexion this affair may assume, it is some consolation to know that neither of the parties implicated are either English or Welsh.

This fear of foreigners stalking the dark streets with knives was a consuming one. It wasn't the Welsh way – though ironically in the same edition, the paper carried the story of a home-grown stabbing in Llangyfelach.

The paper pointed out that it was seven years to the day since Mitropani's death on the Strand. Something had to be done. They had their man and he should be punished.

At the Assizes, the same evidence and the same witnesses were paraded before a jury. The defence argued that the police had been too

eager to secure a conviction. They had
someone, and that was enough for them.
The two witnesses who accused the
Italian sailors could have done it themselves – there was actually no evidence to
suggest they hadn't. The second wound
in the back was a puzzle that no one had
been able to explain.

The jury retired for over an hour and a
half. When they returned, they delivered
a verdict of guilty of murder. There was
considerable surprise in the court, because
it meant that they had chosen to believe
the evidence of two drunken sailors. But

(www.fromoldbooks.org)

there was also a sense that lawlessness amongst sailors must be stopped.
They should not be allowed to resolve their own difficulties down on the
docks in ways that ran counter to the rule of law.

The judge passed a sentence of death and was apparently considerably moved in doing so, unlike Giardinieri, who stood there impassively.
'He heard his doom unmoved, and without the quiver of a muscle.'

Immediately a campaign was started in order to overturn the verdict.
There was overwhelming evidence to show that Giardinieri had been
with Peter Moitch on the night of his death, but none whatsoever to
suggest that he had killed him. A successful campaign was mounted to
commute the death sentence, just days before it was due to be carried out
in August. He was then detained in custody at Her Majesty's pleasure
whilst further enquiries were made. And they were right to do so, because
they had the wrong man entirely. They should have been looking for a
man called Lazauti, who had been on the other side of Moitch and had
disappeared into the night after the stabbing. The others knew it was him,
but were unwilling to implicate him. It was not what honourable Italians
did. His name was apparently revealed during confession in prison to
Revd Chaplain.

On 15 February 1866 Giardinieri received a free pardon. An official letter
from the Secretary of State was read to him in prison, saying that new

evidence had come to light. He was still implicated in the murder, but he was to be released on the understanding that he left England within thirty days and never returned. He was told that he should be thankful that God inspired the Queen with a sentiment of mercy. I am sure he was. He fell to his knees. 'Dio vi benedica, come mi benedice ora a me!'

Before he left forever, he had his photograph taken by the celebrated local photographer Mr Andrews. But Lazauti never showed up to have his photograph taken.

As an interesting postscript to this story, I can tell you that on 6 July 1866 it was reported that the Treasury had refused to allow £128 16s 3d on the bill of costs for the trial, because Swansea had submitted the wrong paper-work. The Clerk of the Peace was told to sort it out as quickly as possible.

CASE TEN 1872

THE GOOD TEMPLAR?

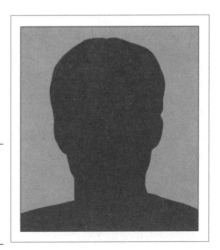

Supect: Andrew Joseph
Duncan

Age: Thirty-two

Charge: Murder

'Andrew Joseph Duncan, blockmaker, was charged with feloniously, wickedly and with malice aforethought, killing and slaying his wife, Emma Duncan, at Swansea on 25 October 1872.'

Andrew Duncan was found at the bottom of Welcome Lane at 6 a.m. He was semi-naked and dripping with water. He had thrown himself into the North Dock to drown, but had then thought better of it and surrendered himself to Police Constable John Lewis. He had, he said, murdered his wife. 'Here,' he said. 'I give myself into your hands.'

He accompanied the policeman to his lodgings, walking calmly alongside him. Duncan was a block and spar maker and he lived with his family upstairs at 25a the Strand, next door to the Crown Inn. Inside was a shocking sight.

The bed was saturated with blood. Emma Duncan lay there, with her fourth child, three months old, asleep at her breast. Her head was a terrible mess. Her skull had been fractured in six places and her brain was protruding, 'the front of her head having been completely broken in'. He had attacked her with a flat iron, which was lying on the floor. There were some

Andrew Duncan's death certificate. (Author's collection)

wounds which may have been caused by a razor which was found beneath the mattress, but her head was such a mess it was hard to be sure. She was still alive, though barely, and died later in the evening in hospital.

Duncan was from Bristol, and his wife Emma came from Llanelli. After their marriage there in 1865, they had four children at roughly two year intervals, moving between Llanelli and Swansea. A reporter described the lodging as

SHOCKING WIFE MURDER IN SWANSEA.

In our last impression we briefly noticed a shocking case of wife murder which occurred in this town that (Friday) morning. About 6 o'clock in the morning a police constable named John Lewis on duty in the Strand, was accosted by a man in a state of semi-nudity and dripping wet, who said that he had a short time previously murdered his wife, that he had subsequently attempted to drown himself in the dock but had failed, and that he now wanted to give himself up to justice. The officer went with the man to a small house pointed out by the latter, and on going upstairs a shocking spectacle presented itself. A woman not yet thirty years of age was lying in bed, with an infant three months old asleep at her breast. The pillow and bed clothes were saturated with blood, there was a pool of blood on the floor, and subsequent medical investigation revealed the fact that the poor creature, lying in bed, had the front of her head completely smashed in, there being on the side of her head, no less than six fearful wounds, from three of which the brain was actually protruding. The woman was still breathing, but unconscious. An ordinary flat iron, such as laundresses use, was lying beside the bed, covered with blood and hair, leaving no doubt as to the weapon with which the fatal injuries had been inflicted. Crimes of violence of this serious character are happily very rare in Swansea, and the tragic occurrence has excited an unusual sensation in the town.

(By kind permission of SWW Media)

having 'a very cheerless and poverty-stricken aspect'. There was little furniture apart from 'two mean beds'. In the other bed their three sons, Andrew, Joseph and Alfred, were crying loudly.

'her brain was protruding'

There were no marks anywhere on her body. There were no signs of a struggle. Doctors suggested that she had been stunned by the first blow and hadn't moved again. There was no doubt what had happened, nor indeed who had done it. Nor was there any doubt about why it happened. Duncan told everyone:

I've killed my wife. There's a hole in the wall and a man from next door was looking through and making faces at my wife. I have cautioned her about it several times before, but she always denied it and at last I saw him and she knew my temper well.

The police checked thoroughly. There was no hole in the wall. Duncan was mad.

At the inquest one of the witnesses was Martha Jones, who slept on the other side of the wall, in The Crown, where she was in service. She had heard cries in the early morning. A woman's voice cried: 'Murder!' and 'O God!'. Martha leaned out of the window and told John Griffiths, who occupied the foundry opposite. He too heard children screaming but continued to be busy opening up his premises. Martha did think of sending her husband to investigate, but he was lying insensible in bed, having been 'on the spree' the previous evening. Thus Emma was left all alone to die.

Duncan didn't say much at the inquest and said little at his trial. He appeared detached from the terrible inevitability of the proceedings. There was no evidence of any provocation. Emma was described as 'a good woman, industrious and attentive to her children'. He hadn't been drunk. Police opinion was that there was nothing wrong with him.

Mental instability was raised by the prosecution as the only possible explanation for his actions. The defence agreed, since there was no motive for such a frenzied assault. However, his problem was that in giving himself up to the police, he seemed to acknowledge that he had done something wrong. Everyone knew that Emma had been murdered. All the jury had to decide was whether Duncan was sane.

The jury retired for about thirty minutes. When they returned, they found him guilty of wilful murder and he was condemned to death. The judge himself could see no possibility of reprieve.

Strenuous efforts were made to obtain clemency from the Secretary of State, though stories emerged that Emma had moved out a couple of times previously because Duncan had ill-treated her. In prison Duncan appeared quite unconcerned.

The *Cambrian* reported that 'the prisoner answers readily and intelligently every question put to him but professes to be quite oblivious of the cause for which he is detained in gaol.'

Duncan insisted that he was being punished for something he hadn't done. His mother and other members of his family visited him in prison, and as *The Western Mail* put it, betrayed considerable emotion on bidding him farewell, though he appeared to be indifferent to all feeling. It seems that prior to the murder he had talked of joining the Swansea branch of the Good Templars (now known as the International Organisation of Good Templars), a temperance group. He had promised to attend a lodge meeting in the Ebenezer Schoolrooms on Ebenezer Street days before the murder, but he never turned up. Perhaps he realised he had a problem, and was looking for a way to deal with it.

Dr Orange, the medical superintendent from Broadmoor, came to see him, and as a result of this assessment he was reprieved. The newspapers took a mixed view of this. The Swansea-based the *Cambrian* was generous: 'Every lover of humanity will have cause for rejoicing at the life of the unhappy man being spared.'

The Western Mail, based in Cardiff, however, was less compassionate. 'Swansea will be spared the great moral lesson which his strangulation would have afforded. The man is mad; or at least – he is deemed to be by the Government mad doctors sent down to examine him.'

What rather exercised people was the fact that a jury listened to the evidence and then found him guilty, whilst two doctors, acting alone, appear to have overruled them. And not only that. Hanging was, on balance, considerably cheaper than paying to maintain Duncan in Broadmoor. He would be costing the authorities 14s a week. Nonetheless, it was to Broadmoor he was dispatched in the middle of April 1873, to be detained at Her Majesty's pleasure.

The children, who had seen things no child should ever have to confront, did not prosper. Alfred was brought up by his grandparents in Llanelli, changing his name to Wilson. The baby, however, disappears from the records completely and does not seem to have survived Emma's death. The eldest, Andrew, died before his father came to trial, and Joseph died in Cardiff in 1874. The family had been effectively destroyed.

Duncan's brother Neil was constantly supportive and campaigned for his release. He was tireless – but then he had to be. On his admission Duncan was described as of intemperate habits. Dr Orange commented: 'When admitted his mind was much deranged and he laboured under delusions of a dangerous character.'

His state of mind slowly improved but it was felt unsafe to discharge him, particularly in the light of what he had done. Neil Duncan offered to look after him in Liverpool. His sister, Mrs A. Huxley, offered to keep him in Bristol. The MP E. Whiteley got involved, for by the hospital's own admission,

Andrew Duncan was 'rational, tranquil, orderly, and industrious' after ten years, a state of mind many of us still quietly envy.

The authorities eventually relented and he was given a conditional discharge into the care of his brother in Liverpool on 4 April 1892. He had been in Broadmoor for nineteen years.

He seemed to be rebuilding a life for himself in Liverpool. He had a place of his own on Whitefields Lane. Neil Duncan said that 'he was full of bright plans and hope for the future ... a kind word and a bright look was what he had for everyone, God bless him'.

But in the evening of 23 January 1893, he left his brother's house in Cochrane Street. What happened next, no one can be sure, but he fell into the Langton Graving Dock, which was quite empty and dry. He died of his injuries in Bootle Hospital. He was fifty-three.

And so the story of Andrew Duncan comes full circle. It started when he pulled himself out of the North Dock in Swansea and ended in a dry dock in Liverpool. Was it an accident? Did he lose his way and stumble on a dark January night? Or was he in some way trying to expiate the guilt he carried with him for the awful murder of his wife?

You choose.

AND SO THIS IS CHRISTMAS, AND WHAT HAVE YOU DONE?

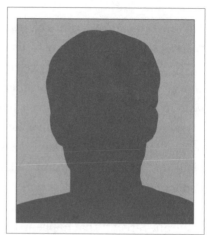

Suspect:	Thomas Howells
Age:	Unknown
Charge:	Murder

David Edwards was a collier from Pyle. He was thirty-five years old and married with two children. On Boxing Day 1873, he and some mates came to Swansea to celebrate the festivities. He stayed that night with his cousin John Bevan in the Ty Melyn public house in High Street. Then after breakfast on Saturday, John went off to see his sister in Sketty whilst Edwards went out on the town. John never saw him alive again.

Edwards had already had two pints of beer with his breakfast, and by midday the pals from Pyle were in the Thistle public house. In the bar there was Thomas Howells, a collier from Swansea. For some reason angry words were exchanged. The landlord, William Jones, knew Howells and asked him to stop. He told him, 'If you cannot come to my house without making a noise, I'd rather you stay away.' The argument continued, although since it was in

(Author's collection)

Welsh, Jones had no idea what it was about. In the end, Jones took the shortest one, who ever he was, by the coat sleeve and escorted him off the premises. The visitors gathered outside and he said, 'There's good fellows, go away.'

They didn't. They just waited for Howells to emerge. When he did come out, he was accosted in Welsh in an angry tone. The short one raised his fist, so Howells knocked him down, and the Swansea boy went on to put

'He fell against the legs of a horse'

up a brave fight. Howells held them all off. The short one got up and took off his hat and coat, so Howells knocked him down again. He turned his attentions to the others, pausing only to knock Shorty to the floor a third time. Clearly plucky, though not gifted.

He then struck Edwards on the nose. He staggered backwards, and lost his footing when he stepped off the kerb. He fell against the legs of a horse tethered to a coal cart, and slipped underneath. Being restive and unsettled by the disturbance close at hand, the horse pranced for a moment and stood on Edwards' stomach. Howells quickly grabbed his legs and dragged him clear. Edwards' nose was bleeding, but he said nothing and walked off into nearby Williams Court. Sergeant Coward of the Swansea Police, attracted by the disturbance, had arrived and followed him. He found Edwards sitting in a chair, being attended. Someone was washing his face but he seemed quite insensible. Coward tried to give him some brandy on a spoon, but he couldn't swallow it. He was immediately carried to a cab and Coward took him to the hospital.

Dr Lloyd, the house surgeon, attended to him. He noted that he smelt strongly of drink. He opened his clothes and ordered hot water bottles for his feet. All that could be seen was the mark of a blow on the nose and a slight bruise on the stomach. But all was in vain. Fifteen minutes after being admitted Edwards died, for his liver had been ruptured.

The post-mortem showed that the liver was completely lacerated and the blood vessels divided. The abdomen was full of blood.

Howells gave himself up almost immediately to Inspector Staddon in Back Street, saying, 'I knocked the man down in High Street.' Of course he maintained that he had been acting in self-defence: 'Three men came up to me and speaking Welsh asked me if I wanted to fight. I said no, you are too many against one.'

The magistrates blamed drinking for the death – the curse of the country. The hoof of the horse was the agent that caused death but Howells hitting Edwards on the nose was the primary cause – the result of the unlawful act of fighting. Consequently Howells had to stand trial on the charge of 'feloniously killing and slaying David Edwards'.

You sense though that this was a formality. Everyone agreed about what had happened. It was unfortunate indeed, but Howells was as much victim as he was villain. There was evidence to suggest that the men from Pyle had set upon him. He had never intended to murder anyone; indeed, he had dragged the poor Edwards away from the horse after thumping him. The evidence was considered once again at the Assizes in March, after which Howells was found not guilty.

On being discharged he made a small bow to the court and left.

CASE TWELVE 1874

BREAD OF HEAVEN

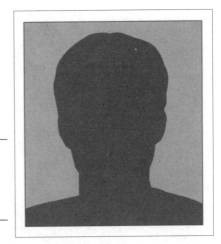

Suspect:	Emanuel Godin
Age:	Twenty-seven
Charge:	Murder

Perhaps after too long on board ship, he felt the need to add to the local gene pool. Or perhaps he was attracted by an unfamiliar range of lamp posts. Either way, the disappearance of the ship's dog precipitated a sudden and completely unnecessary death.

A small French schooner from Bordeaux called the *Nouvelle Anais* had been moored on the South Dock for almost three weeks and was ready to return with a cargo of coal. Hence the anxiety about the dog.

There was a crew of four. The captain Emanuel Godin (twenty-seven years of age), Emile Droual, the mate, seventeen-year-old Pierre Forgue, able seaman, and the cabin boy Fernand Martin, who was sixteen. As you might imagine on a voyage on a small vessel, relationships could become tense and frayed. For some reason, Godin and Forgue had not got on very well. Perhaps they were all rather young. Perhaps there was a lack of respect. Certainly Godin stopped Forgue's grog ration as punishment at some stage.

On the night of 22 July 1874 Godin took Forgue and Martin ashore to look for the dog, but they couldn't find it. He went back to the ship, telling the two boys to continue the search. They do not appear to have fancied it too much, and by eleven o'clock they had had enough. They borrowed a boat from another ship and rowed back to the *Nouvelle Anais*. Godin had been eating some bread in his cabin, and was not too pleased to see them. He said they should stay ashore all night. He slapped Pierre on the cheek so hard that Martin got back into the rowing boat, afraid that it might be his turn next.

(Author's collection)

The disagreement continued for quite some time. Emile Droual, who was below, heard them but saw nothing. Then Godin pushed Pierre hard in the chest, in an attempt to move him away. Pierre was a big boy – bigger than Godin – and so he used both hands. He still had his bread in his hand – and more crucially – the knife he had been cutting it with. Godin probably forgot that it was there. But Godin could not have had a deadlier aim if he had tried a thousand times. It slipped easily between Pierre's ribs and travelled 4in to bury itself in his heart.

'Oh capitaine, vous m'avez donné un mauvais coup.' He said no more.

It was all over in an instant. There was no plan, no murderous intention. Just a momentary loss of temper, with horrific consequences. The *Cambrian* later reported: 'A ghastly spectacle presented itself – immediately over the region of the heart was a deep thrust, a clean-cut incised wound, about an inch wide, but apparently very deep ...'

Droual went up on deck to see what was happening. There was blood. Lots of it. It was spurting out of the wound. Pierre fell into his arms. Droual tried to bandage the wound, first with a handkerchief and then with a shirt.

Godin asked to be kept informed of Pierre's condition and retired to his cabin. But after twenty minutes, Pierre's pulse faded and disappeared, and he was suddenly very cold. In the morning it took a while to wash the blood off the deck. Emile Droual didn't like to see it.

Godin went to the police himself: 'Something amiss has happened on board, and I now have a sailor lying dead.' They knew nothing of this death until Godin reported it. The problem was that he kept changing his story. Everything seemed confusing. The crew's English was limited, and so their story was a little difficult for the police to put together. They relied on an interpreter, William D'Austein, a ship broker's clerk in Swansea, but the police throughout felt dangerously distanced from the facts of the case.

Godin had originally told Droual that Pierre had been drinking, and had fallen and hurt himself on something protruding from the deck. Now he told the police that one of his crew had been stabbed on shore, under one

'A ghastly spectacle presented itself'

of the dark arches. According to the captain, Pierre had come back on a boat borrowed from another vessel, and then collapsed and died on deck. This was quickly dismissed. A man, even someone as large and strong and healthy as Pierre, would have been unable to climb up the side of the ship with such a wound in his chest. Godin was arrested and charged with murder, which he continued to deny.

He was eventually tried in March 1875. He had been waiting in prison for eight months. When the charge of murder was made, he replied in a loud voice, 'I did it innocently.' It was clear that the murder charge was difficult to sustain. There appeared to be no motive, no malice; just a loss of temper. Godin hadn't produced the knife. It was already in his hand because he was using it. The blow was due to 'the frailty of human nature'. The jury found him guilty of manslaughter. Since he had already been in prison for eight months, he was sentenced to six months' imprisonment with hard labour.

The fate of the dog is not recorded.

CASE THIRTEEN   1881

'I HAVE KILLED MY LILY'

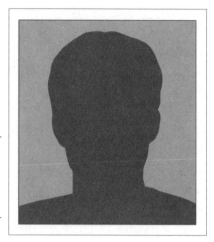

Suspect:	Joseph Boyce
Age:	Thirty-one
Charge:	Murder

I have researched many stories in the writing of this book. Most have been sad; some have been tragic. But nothing has touched me as deeply as the tragic story of Joseph Boyce and his daughter Rosannah Lillian.

It is a remarkable story in so many different ways, which will leave you horrified, shocked and possibly with a sense of disbelief.

The Western Mail, in the first flush of horror at the death of the little girl, was ready to describe it as 'one of the most revolting murders ever perpetrated in the town'. Perhaps it was.

It happened during the afternoon of Monday 22 August 1881 at the family home at 2 Williams Court on High Street – where the injured David Edwards had been taken in 1873. Joseph Boyce came from Warwick, though he had previously lived in London and Hereford. He was working as a watchman or

'one of the most revolting murders ever perpetrated in the town'

policeman on the railway, and he was thirty-one years old. He lived with his wife and his daughter Lily, who was two years and eight months old. He had, apparently, always shown 'the greatest fondness for his daughter'. He was regarded as 'a sober man and a good husband'. Everyone said that he loved his child. But that Monday afternoon, something happened; something snapped inside him and the world was never the same again.

It had been an argumenta-
tive sort of afternoon. He had
quarrelled initially with his
brother-in-law, William Lewis,
who was unemployed. Joseph
thought that his wife was giving
her brother money. There was
almost a fight.

Mrs Boyce calmed things down,
sent her brother away, and went
outside just after 3 p.m. to shake
a mat.

When she came back, she found
Lily standing between Joseph's
knees. There was a deep wound to
her skull made with the hatchet
that Joseph used for chopping
firewood. Hannah McQueen,

(Author's collection)

who lived opposite, heard Mrs Boyce screaming and saw her carrying out
Lily with blood streaming from her head. Joseph had the hatchet in his hand.
When she spoke to him, he said nothing. She said, 'You have killed your little
child with a hatchet.' He still said nothing.

Another neighbour, Anne Rees, came, drawn by the screams. She saw
Joseph sitting on a chair by the front door. He was staring at the floor,
looking wild and strange. 'I have killed my Lily,' he said.

The police were called. PC Johns found Boyce sitting in a chair,
smoking a cigar. He expressed some surprise that the police were there.
When Johns picked up the hatchet from the floor, Boyce asked if he
could have it back.

He was taken to High Street, and when charged with attempting to
murder his daughter by striking her on the head with a hatchet, he said,
'I know nothing about it.' And then he said something that was most unexpected. It was brief exchange, but one which characterises the case.

He asked, 'Is my little girl dead?'

When PC Coker said no, he replied, 'I wish she was.'

These words were repeatedly analysed. What did he mean? Did they give some insight into his mental state? Were they callous? Or were they compassionate? They were words which did not clarify the situation; they merely added to the confusion.

Poor Lily lived for a few hours but died shortly after six o'clock. When Joseph was told that he was to be charged with her murder, he seemed genuinely shocked. 'Good God. My child is dead?'

The police went back to check the house, and on the floor PC Johns found one of Lily's fingers that had been chopped off. How had this happened? Had she put her hand up to protect herself? Could there be any other explanation?

Joseph Boyce appeared in court in November 1881, vilified across the country for his apparent crime. He was seen as a monster, a cruel and brutal murderer. He was described as standing 'in an awful position between life and death'. Lily's life had been destroyed in a wilful act, and now his own life hung in the balance.

And yet, did anyone really know what had happened?

No one saw Lily's death. No motive could be determined. There was no evidence of murder. It could have happened accidentally. Joseph could have thrown the hatchet which hit her accidentally. She could have thrown it in the air. Nothing was clear, and Joseph insisted throughout that he had no recollection of what had happened. Those bizarre words, 'I wish she was,' were carefully examined. What did they mean? That he wanted her dead? Or that he wanted her released from her suffering? Nothing about the case seemed to make any sense. So, guided by the judge, Lord Justice Lush, the jury retired for fifteen minutes and returned a verdict of not guilty. Joseph Boyce, 'a man of irreproachable character', was acquitted and released.

Within the limits of their understanding at that time, what choice was there? Today, there would have been more informed investigations into Joseph's condition, but without a motive or witnesses it seemed impossible to explain.

Perhaps the argument caused some kind of fit. How can we know? Everyone said that he appeared drunk, even though he hadn't been drinking. His brother-in-law stated that 'he seemed to bend down all on one side and his eye seemed to be fixed'. A neighbour, Mr Williams, noted that 'there was a wild look about his eyes'. Anne Rees said that she had heard he was subject to epileptic fits.

Mrs Boyce said he'd fallen out of a train in Hereford. That he had once been bitten by a dog. That he hadn't been sleeping. They were desperate to find some context that could explain the horror that had taken place. They were trying to explain the inexplicable. Perhaps there was some kind of storm in his head, some kind of fit. They didn't know.

But little Lily died horribly and it was beyond reason.

The story continued to haunt me; I found a similar case from October 1937. Edwin Warlow, from Jericho Row in Foxhole, killed his six-month-old son, Ronald, with three blows to the head with a hatchet. Edwin was convinced of his own criminality. He believed that, together with his entirely imaginary friend Patsy Carroll, he had spent the wages of all his colleagues at the oil works. As a result he had been forced to kill his own son Ronald.

Edwin was declared 'insane and detained until his Majesty's pleasure be known'.

CASE FOURTEEN 1884

APRIL FOOL

Suspect:	Josiah Padley
Age:	Forty-seven
Charge:	None

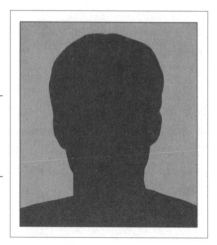

The house in High Street stank of fish. That is what the reporters first noticed – 'salt fish mingling in a sickly way with smells from the dwelling itself' and with those from the backyard where the animals were kept. A fit place for an intensive investigation by the local board of health, is what they thought. But that could wait. The reporters were there to see the bodies; those of Josiah and Jane Padley.

But they were warned – the house was dilapidated, there was little furniture, and the rickety stairs may not take their weight.

There is a sense of poverty and squalor running through this story – unhappiness, waste, dirt, futility. And madness.

The shed leaning against the rear of the house had beams from which herring were hung for drying. It was here that Josiah had hanged himself. There was a new rope around his neck, intended to repair a fisherman's net. He had jumped off some steps, and since he was a heavy man, death appeared to have been instantaneous. In death Josiah appeared calm, his 'good features' untroubled by the horror he had left behind.

Josiah had decided in November 1883 that something had to be done, either to himself or his wife, on 1 April 1884. He had warned the police that something would happen. He told an acquaintance, Henry Marle, that Jane was trying to poison him but that '1 April would settle it all'. And so at midnight on 31 March 1884 he wrote a letter and then murdered Jane.

She was forty-seven and the mother of seventeen children, of whom only seven were still living. You might think that there had been enough sadness in her life already. But Josiah was a jealous man.

The *Cambrian* newspaper tells us that 'It seems extraordinary that after living with her for twenty-seven years, Padley should have such suspicions of her conduct'.

But he did. And she paid for them.

They had lived at 171–172 High Street for twelve years. It was almost directly opposite the police station, on the corner of Pottery Street. Josiah was a fishmonger and had an extensive and lucrative trade in fish, potatoes and vegetables. He was, however, 'improvident in his habits'. Josiah was 'addicted to heavy drinking', and was sometimes violent. Jane did her best to keep the business operating, and had on occasion moved out, taking the youngest children with her. In fact, he had been bound over to keep the peace about a month previously. The police had often been called. His mother-in-law, Mary Harris, said that he had not been properly sober for nine years.

But there had been a sense of foreboding in the air. Josiah had talked to the servant Emma Jenkins repeatedly about 1 April. That was when he would 'do it'. He told Mary Harris that he would do it on 1 April but never explained what that might be. He told his son-in-law that 'The first of April will tell all.'

Arguments were common. On one occasion Jane had thrown turnips at him and had accused him, ironically perhaps, of infidelity.

That evening he had seemed neither excited nor drunk. Relationships appeared to be quite cordial. He had come home from work, sat down and read the paper. Rather ominously, he had been very keen to tell his daughter Victoria and the servant Emma about two men who were about to be hanged. Then Josiah wrote his letter to the coroner on business memorandum forms. The letter was dated midnight 1 April 1884.

> This is to certify that I, Josiah, the once happy husband of Jane Padley until the Brothers Ley seduced her, then I could not have any rest with her, drunk nor sober. It is through they I got the three months in prison for breaking a few articles, not for striking her with an hatchet this is my last word we have had words tonight.

Victoria had indeed heard them arguing, though nothing too serious. In fact he appeared to be on 'unusually friendly terms' with her mother. Then, in the night, Josiah had entered her room and put an envelope under her

(Author's collection)

pillow, saying, 'There's a letter.' He went back to his room and there were sounds as if he was beating something. He returned to Victoria's room and put an unlit candle on the table. She asked him what was wrong. 'Nothing,' he said, and went downstairs. There was silence, apart from the sound of what she thought was her mother snoring.

Victoria called out to her father after about forty-five minutes, but there was no reply. She was frightened. It didn't seem right. Emma looked in the bedroom and then called for a policeman.

Jane was lying on her bed, with deep cuts to her head. Her skull had been smashed. She was still alive when she was taken to the hospital but never recovered consciousness and died twenty-four hours later.

Victoria's sister Hilda shared their parents' bedroom. She had seen Josiah with a black-handled knife in his hands, as well as a small crowbar. When he saw Hilda looking, he put out the candle. But she was there.

Jane suffered five wounds to her head. The left temple was smashed in. A blow to the forehead had broken through the skull to the brain.

In the opinion of the *Cambrian*, 'there was only one possible verdict: that

'Her skull had been smashed'

Jane died by wilful murder at the hand of her husband, and that Josiah Padley committed suicide whilst suffering from temporary insanity.'

James and George Ley were potato merchants, and they were anxious to vindicate themselves, having been directly accused in Padley's letter, which *The Western Mail* had seen fit to publish. Of course they denied any involvement. When Padley had started to talk of horror in April, they had actually been in Australia and had not returned until January. They believed that he had invented the story because the Leys refused to do business with him and preferred to work with Jane. This might well have bred suspicion, but it was very simple: Josiah wouldn't pay. He owed them a considerable amount of money. Jane traded on her own account, selling vegetables. And so she paid a heavy price.

CASE FIFTEEN 1885

'KISS ME, JULIA'

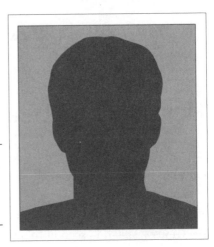

Suspect:	Walter Jenkins
Age:	Twenty-three
Charge:	Manslaughter

Poor William Smith, 'a man of peaceful habits'. He and his wife Mary had come down from Yorkshire and set up in business as bakers and confectioners. He was sixty-nine, 'healthy and well nourished, with a tendency towards corpulence'. And he was shot and murdered by his assistant Walter Jenkins at his shop on Llangyfelach Street on 15 August 1885.

In court, Jenkins took his time climbing into the dock. After all, he was still weak from his self-inflicted wounds and he looked rather pale. He seemed respectable, though the reporter from the *Cambrian* was not impressed by his appearance. He had a 'small forehead, a retreating chin and a mouth which would be regarded as cruel'.

Jenkins had been the manager of the shop. He was twenty-three. Respected. Trusted. A man of high character. His previous employer, Mr West of High Street, said so. But no one could know what was seething inside his head. And if I tell you that the business had another branch in Swansea Market, and that it was run by Julia Clarke who was seventeen, and that they both lodged with the Smiths, you might anticipate the outlines of this sad story.

Mary and Julia came home late from Saturday's business in the market, and were surprised to find a rather irritable carrier called Merrill waiting impatiently. He had arrived with a bill for flour, but no one would deal with him.

They soon found out why. Jenkins was lying on the floor in the parlour with his arms over his head. 'Shake hands with me and let me die,' he said to Mary. He was bleeding from the nose and mouth, and when asked where William was, he replied, 'He is in the kitchen, dead. I shot him.'

William was lying on the floor, with his head and shoulders against the wall. He had been shot once, on the left side of the chest, straight through the heart.

'Shake hands with me and let me die'

Jenkins appeared rational. He wouldn't take any brandy, because he wanted to die. He had shot himself in the left side. He said that God would have mercy on his soul.

It was hard to know what could have provoked such an outrage. Jenkins had recently expressed a wish to leave his job. He had been treated as one of the family. Mary had been 'like a mother to him'. But he had handed in his notice, claiming he couldn't put up with William any longer. What that meant, no one could be sure. William had recently scolded him about being too trusting, by offering too much credit to other traders, but nothing more than that. But suddenly, earlier in the week, Jenkins had asked Mary whether her husband believed in God.

On the morning of the murder, Jenkins had been down to the market stall and he seemed fine. Julia asked him to send down more cakes, since they had sold out, and so he had gone back to arrange this.

What happened next isn't clear, but in the early evening, William was shot at close quarters whilst in the kitchen.

Walter was a regular at Carmarthen Road Chapel, which Julia also attended. He spent his time praying in his bedroom, quoting scripture loudly and writing sermons. Perhaps she inspired within him emotions he felt he should control. Yes, they were friendly, but not engaged. Perhaps Walter yearned for more. Perhaps unrequited love gnawed away at him.

Because you see, the first thing he said when they found him was not that request to Mary to shake his hand. His very first words were 'Kiss me, Julia', which, to be honest, was not such an attractive prospect given the amount of blood there was.

And where had he got the gun from? Mary said she would have forbidden it in the house had she known about it. He had bought a revolver and

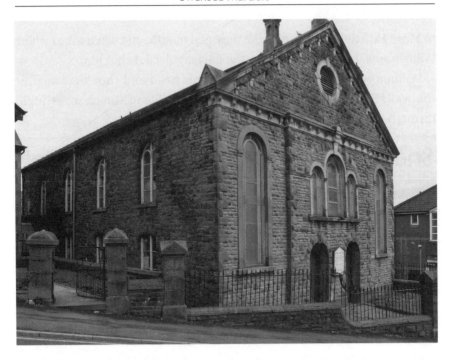

Where Walter Jenkins went to chapel on Carmarthen Road. (Author's collection)

fifty rounds of ammunition from John Beynon, the ironmonger in Castle Square, on Thursday 13 August. Beynon was initially reluctant to admit to the sale, but another customer, the plumber William Northam, remembered the transaction very clearly, since Jenkins had haggled about the price. Northam also remembered Beynon showing Jenkins how to use it. The weight of the evidence refreshed Beynon's memory.

When the case came before the court in November 1885, Walter pleaded not guilty. He argued that he had intended to take his own life, and that William had tried to stop him. They had struggled and the gun had gone off twice. One shot missed; one hit William. He then shot himself. There were suicide notes in his pocket.

One was for his mother, for whom he was the sole support. 'Sorrow has overcome me and I cannot live any longer.'

His letter to Julia said, 'I can endure this no longer.'

The one he wrote to William contained the interesting suggestion that William's 'bad conduct had filled Julia's heart with sorrow'. At the inquest, he retracted any suggestion that there had ever been an improper relationship between his boss and Julia.

He had wanted to carry his secret passion to his grave. He was very sorry for what had happened. He had never intended to harm anyone else. The defence counsel said that his mind had been 'warped by mental depression'.

The court decided that he was not guilty of murder. There was no clear motive. But he was guilty of manslaughter. The judge, Justice Manisty, sentenced him to fifteen years' penal servitude.

CASE SIXTEEN   1885

SAFE IN THE ARMS OF JESUS

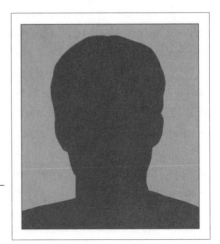

Suspect:	Thomas Nash
Age:	Thirty-nine
Charge:	Murder

Poor Martha Nash.

The English Baptist Band of Hope led the funeral procession to St David's Church in Llangyfelach. As they left the house, they played 'Safe in the Arms of Jesus'. Tragically, Martha hadn't been safe in the hands of her father.

The charge which was said to hang over the head of Thomas Nash, according to the *Cambrian*, is one of 'a peculiarly heinous character. It is that of wilful murder – the murder of his own child. Martha was a young, innocent, inoffensive and helpless infant – a child of only six years of age.'

As we look at the facts of this wretched case, we can see that whatever Nash did or did not do, he was a confused and desperate man. The case appears to be a simple one. He walked onto Swansea pier, hand-in-hand with his daughter, in a storm, and he returned almost immediately without her. She was washed up, drowned, on the beach a couple of hours later. There were no witnesses, but no one worried too much about that. Everyone believed they knew what he had done.

Nash, originally from Castle Martin in Pembrokeshire, had done a number of jobs and lived in a number of places as he worked hard to support his family. In the 1881 census he is described as a furnaceman.

By 1885, he was working as a labourer for Swansea Corporation and living in Graham Street in Hafod. Most importantly, he had been widowed a few years earlier. His wife Martha had died, leaving him to care for two daughters: seventeen-year-old Sarah, and Martha Ann, who was six.

They lodged with Eliza Goodwin for about three years; but in early November 1885, Nash moved out of the lodgings without saying where he was going, leaving his children behind. He popped back one night when Eliza was out to collect his things, but showed no interest in settling his outstanding bill, which was accumulating steadily. Sarah didn't have any regular work so the children and Eliza were in a bit of a fix. Eliza told the court: 'On the following Tuesday after he left I saw the accused passing the house in a cart and I called him into the house and asked him when he was going to fetch the children and pay me. He said he would come and fetch the children that evening but he never came.'

Eliza kept on looking after the girls, but was getting irritated by Nash's evasions. She then saw him on the road to Morriston, and again he said

(Author's collection)

he would come to fetch the girls. She told him, 'I can't possibly afford to keep them. It is more than I can do.'

Eventually she decided to take matters into her own hands.

Friday 5 December 1885 was payday for Corporation workers, and Eliza took Martha down to the Town Hall. Confronting Nash at the pay office, she gave him two things – his daughter and a bill for £1 16s 2d. He promised he would pay the bill on Saturday.

'Shall I come home with you, Mrs Goodwin?' asked Martha.

'No, my dear. You must go with your father.'

That was the last time Eliza ever saw Martha alive.

Nash's problem was more complicated than mere money. He'd moved out in order to get married to twenty-seven-year-old Margaret on 16 November 1885. And he hadn't told Margaret that he had any children.

Obviously he had no idea how to deal with the situation in which he found himself. It would have been one thing to suddenly reveal a daughter called Sarah who was now out at work. But it would be something else entirely to produce a little six-year old, dressed in 'a little red turn-over, straw hat, pinafore'. The *Cambrian* loved such atmospheric detail, but of course Martha was not the sort of detail that you could forget.

It was a wild night, with a howling wind and waves crashing over the pier, as all the witnesses would testify. Nash left the pay office and walked hand-in-hand with Martha onto Swansea pier. The tide was high.

Two men, Owen and Fender, were watching.

'We thought it was strange to see a man and child out on the pier on such a night.'

Then moments later they saw Nash alone, jumping down a 14ft drop onto the sand.

They asked after the child.

'She is on the top,' he said.

If this was the case, then why had he left her there? Fender and Owen decided they should keep hold of him until the police arrived.

Nash then said that he'd left Martha under the pier.

Suspicions were aroused, especially when Nash himself tried to walk into the sea. They restrained him and Nash became silent and would not speak.

When PC Davies arrived, Nash changed his story once again. He now said he'd put Martha on the rail of the pier in order to carry her on his back, and she had fallen off. Then he became silent again.

A short while later they found her, drowned, close by the bathing machines.

There was nothing much else to say. Nash was arrested and searched. In his pocket they found 19s 6d and Eliza's bill.

The due processes of the law dissected the details minutely, but there was little else to be revealed.

Throughout the proceedings Nash said nothing, 'maintaining a dejected attitude'. He 'clasped his cap in his hands and kept his eyes down upon the front rail of the dock'. There was no one to speak for him. The only person

'Nash himself tried to walk into the sea'

who showed any sympathy towards him was Sarah ('a clean, tidy and respectable-looking girl'), who cried bitterly and tried to comfort him, but Thomas Nash had drawn completely into himself.

Whether he threw little Martha off the pier or not, his reactions to her disappearance condemned him. He hadn't beaten her – there were no marks on her body – but if he had wanted to put her on his back, he could either have lifted her directly or used the seats on the pier. He had shown no alarm when first confronted about her disappearance, and had then given conflicting accounts.

It was murder. He was guilty. He was condemned to death.

There can be no doubt that he was bewildered by the position he found himself in, and his behaviour in court would support this.

Who can really say what happened? Perhaps he did sit her on the rail whilst desperately seeking a solution in his mind, and she fell off. His explanation is so feeble that it could quite possibly have been true. But he did write a letter to *The Western Mail* which was published a few days before his execution, in which he confessed to the murder: 'The sentence that was passed on me was only what I really did deserve, for I did do it wilfully.'

We can never know whether that was the truth – or horrible guilt.

Attempts to win a reprieve were doomed, given the nature of his crime. That picture of a little girl dead on the beach was sufficient. There were

Llangyfelach Cemetery, where Martha rests. (Author's collection)

petitions organised by Revd Snelling – there were always petitions when anyone was executed, for the death sentence aroused strong opposition – but few signatories.

Throughout his imprisonment Thomas Nash received no visitors other than Sarah. His new wife seems to have vanished. He was a lost and abandoned man.

He was hanged on Monday 1 March 1886, with an estimated crowd of 4,000 waiting outside Swansea Prison for the black flag to be hoisted, despite a heavy snowfall overnight.

Poor Martha was destined for a pauper's grave until the neighbours stepped in. The *Cambrian* newspaper tells us that 'In every sphere of life there beat some noble hearts.' Those who had known Martha Ann's mother rallied round. Mrs Miles and Mrs Boys collected the money and Mrs Davies, who lived opposite the grocer Mr Lewis, 'took the little corpse into her house ... where dozens of the children who had known the deceased took occasion to look at her in her little coffin where she lay more as if sleeping than the victim of a fearful tragedy.' She then went by procession to Llangyfelach church where she was buried with her mother.

'I COULD NOT STOP MYSELF'

Suspect:	David Davies
Age:	Twenty-five
Charge:	Murder

David Davies was twenty-five years old. He was a seaman – 'a stalwart, clear-eyed and good-looking fellow'. He had been married to his attractive twenty-year-old wife Mary Jane for over two years. And he murdered her by slashing her throat with a razor.

They lived with Mary Jane's mother, the widow Gwenllian Walters, and her five other children, at 6 Hall Street in Waun Wen. She worked as a 'butcheress' in Swansea Market, and Mary Jane worked as her assistant. On the morning of Tuesday 6 February 1888, Gwenllian was awoken by screams and the word 'Murder!' echoing through the house. There were two bedrooms. She shared one with five of her children, and Mary Jane and David had the other. And that is where the noise seemed to be coming from.

Inside she found her daughter by the bed, desperately clutching her throat, which was bleeding terribly. David pushed past her, dressed only in his trousers. She chased after him and grabbed him in the kitchen; they struggled

'desperately clutching her throat'

briefly until he got away. The only thing she remembered him saying was 'Leave me go, for God's sake, to give myself up.' There was blood on his hands. Mary Jane appeared too, but she was taken back upstairs.

Davies ran off down Baptist Well Street. 'He seemed terrified, like someone out of his mind,' said a neighbour who saw him. Back in Hall Street, all was chaotic. The Walters children were screaming, and Mrs Baker came over

Hall Street, Swansea, 2012. (Author's collection)

to help. She found Mary Jane upstairs and gently raised her head, but the blood just rushed out. Another neighbour, William Phillips, came to help too. He also lifted up her head. He too watched the blood pour from the horrible slash across her throat. She died before the doctor came. When he arrived, he commented that she had the body 'of a well-nourished woman'; apart, of course, from the gaping wound in her neck.

Meanwhile Davies arrived at the police station on High Street, carrying with him splashes of his wife's blood on his hands and clothes. He gave himself up. 'For killing my wife,' he said. 'I cut her throat with a razor.' He was described as 'sober but very excited'.

There was little that he could say. The previous night they had both been out separately. Mary Jane had gone to pay the rent, to collect her younger sisters from a concert at the Royal Standard, and then to call on an aunt. Everything seemed fine. There were no arguments, and they gave every impression of being a contented couple. He had in fact been 'quite friendly with her'.

But something was wrong. Horribly wrong.

The inquest was held in the Waunwen Inn in Cwmbwrla. There could be no argument about what had happened. When he was taken away to custody at the end of the inquest, boys followed the cab down Carmarthen Road, hooting and yelling.

The *Cambrian* newspaper reported that 'on Sunday the house in which the deceased lay was crowded with visitors, everyone whose morbid curiosity brought them to the door being allowed to enter.'

Mary Jane was buried in Cockett Cemetery and many attended, in spite

THE SWANSEA MURDER.—The body of the deceased woman, Mary Jane Davies, who died at the hands of her husband last week, was interred at Cockett Church on Monday afternoon. In spite of the snowstorm, there was a large attendance at the suburban Churchyard, the deceased being very well known as a dealer at the Swansea Market. It is stated that Josiah Williams, the prisoner's brother-in-law, is getting together subscriptions for the prisoner's defence, and the strange fact that considerable sympathy is felt in the town towards the prisoner is proved by the subscriptions coming in comparatively freely. On Sunday, the house in which deceased lay was crowded with visitors, everyone whose morbid curiosity brought them to the door being allowed to enter.

(By kind permission of SWW Media)

of a snowstorm. Meanwhile, David's brother-in-law, Josiah Williams, who had married his sister, collected contributions for his defence.

In the Magistrates' Court the defence suggestion that Mary Jane's injury was self-inflicted was laughable. Josiah did his best for him. He said that Davies was unhappy because Mary Jane wouldn't leave her mother's house. In fact, according to him, they had once lived apart and he'd moved in with Josiah for about three months. He also claimed that he'd seen Mary Jane arm in arm with another man about eighteen months previously near the station. Josiah's wife – Davies' sister – had allegedly said to her, 'Mary Jane, is this the way you are serving my brother when he is ploughing the sea?' She had laughed and walked on.

A friend, George Mitchell, confirmed the story about Davies wanting to leave Gwen Walters' house. Mary Jane had said that her mother believed that if they moved out he would start to ill-use her. Davies had become so depressed that he had told George he was considering suicide. The general opinion was that his grievance was against his mother-in-law, not his wife.

When the case appeared at the Assizes at Cardiff, Davies was described as 'despondent and melancholy'. New evidence was presented. When he had been staying with Josiah he'd behaved strangely, silently sitting all day in a chair, isolated in his own world.

The key witness was a Dr Pringle, superintendent of the County Lunatic Asylum in Bridgend. He'd examined Davies on a number of occasions. He indicated that Davies had been hearing voices.

Prior to the murder, he hadn't been sleeping. He had heard shouting or whispering. It had been happening in his cell too. On the morning of the murder, he had heard a rustling noise. When he had woken Mary Jane to tell her, she had understandably told him to go back to sleep. He had occasionally felt 'peculiar'. He described a feeling of 'dizziness, accompanied by a darkness or dimness'. He also felt an overwhelming impulse 'to rush at someone'. He had felt like this at sea, and it hadn't gone away. Dr Pringle felt he was epileptic.

He claimed he had no memory of killing her.

'I loved her very much. I couldn't help killing her. She never gave me any cause, but I could not help killing her. I could not stop myself.'

His family history was important too, for there was a belief that mental instability ran in families. He had three sisters with difficulties: one was in the asylum, one was 'an idiot' and he had married the third. 'My wife is a sister to the prisoner. I have to be careful with her, even now.' It was all the father's fault apparently; he was a drunkard. Clearly it was not the healthiest gene pool. David Davies was unwittingly carrying his own share of a family curse.

Dr Pringle's professional opinion was the key. The conclusion was inevitable. He was pronounced 'guilty but insane'. He was detained as a 'criminal lunatic' and immediately admitted to Broadmoor.

He was released in 1898 but found the outside world far too difficult. He was quickly readmitted to Broadmoor and he died there in 1912.

WHEN YOU'RE IN LOVE WITH A BEAUTIFUL WOMAN ...

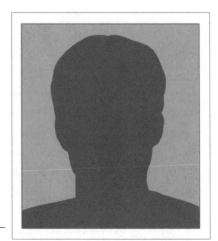

Suspect: Edward Phillips
Age: Thirty-two
Charge: Manslaughter

As you read through this book, you might start to form the impression that being a wife in Swansea was not all it is cracked up to be. You appear to have had every chance of ending up dead. Just like Claire Phillips.

In this story, jealousy is the key.

The press were particularly engaged with the whole tragedy. It wasn't anything to do with sailors. It wasn't committed in 'the most ignorant classes of society'. No. It happened in an apparently ordinary family, at midnight on Friday 7 April 1893.

Edward Phillips was thirty-two years old. He came from a respected family, 'to which one would look at the very last for a murderer'. But he was consumed by jealousy and madness. He was in love with a beautiful woman. And it was hard.

He had married Claire Hyacinthe Ducable, who had worked as a barmaid in three public houses. Her dark complexion and vivacious manners gave her the exotic appeal of a foreigner and encouraged custom. Her father, Pierre, was French, and Claire had been brought up in Newport. Phillips had met her when she was barmaid in the St Ives Inn on Caer Street. They married in St David's Catholic Church in Swansea.

After the marriage Edward set up business as an undertaker in Cemetery Road, St Thomas. Soon there were two children, Hyacinthe May and Percy.

Edward Phillips. (Original illustration by Angela Warne-Payne, based on a contemporary sketch)

And then he started to drink. And it was the drink that 'unseated his reason'.

He drank heavily, to the dismay of his friends. His behaviour became erratic, which has never been the sort of characteristic which identifies the most successful undertakers. In fact, his friends began to question his sanity. Soon the business was in difficulty.

Claire was a temperate, pleasant, kind girl, and she was ready to do whatever she needed to do to sustain the family in the face of her husband's difficulties. But this determination and energy contributed fatally to Edward's insecurities.

They decided to take over the Troubadour Inn, which the press described as a mean little pub. It was at the bottom of Anchor Court on the Strand. Perhaps it was the world that Claire knew best. Perhaps in this way she could keep the family together. Her experience would make the business a success, especially with the number of French sailors visiting Swansea. However, given Edward's problems, it might not have been the wisest decision.

He continued to drink, and the drink made him 'unreasonably suspicious and quarrelsome'. He began to accuse Claire of infidelity and 'kindred vice'. Her job behind the bar required her to be pleasant to strangers, and thus made her vulnerable to the 'merest chimeras of the imagination'. He accused her of becoming violent.

Obviously the relationship became increasingly strained. Storms were gathering inside his head, and they broke horribly when Claire refused to give him any more to drink.

The only witness to the awful events was Mary Howard, who was sixteen years old and in service with the Phillips family. Mary had worked with them for two months. She reported that Edward ate little and drank a lot. They had

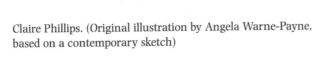

Claire Phillips. (Original illustration by Angela Warne-Payne, based on a contemporary sketch)

The Troubadour. (By kind permission of SWW Media)

been in the Troubadour for two weeks and it wasn't going well.

Friday 7 April 1893 was their fourth wedding anniversary and Claire's twenty-eighth birthday.

Claire and Edward were both working in the bar, but he was increasingly unhappy about the attention she received from male customers. He said loudly that she seemed to be anxious for their attentions. He played cards with an engine driver called Thomas Bowen, drinking whisky and sherry and criticising his wife.

They then argued in the kitchen, and Mary saw him grab Claire by the hair and force her head down onto the table. She tried to pull him away, saying, 'Oh Mr Phillips, don't be so foolish.' He released her, but a short while later instructed Mary to close the house.

Claire ran into Mary's bedroom and closed the door, but Edward told Mary to open it and fetch a light. Whilst Mary was downstairs she heard a struggle and a scream. She ran back upstairs and struck a match. In the feeble light she saw Edward holding a white-handled pocket knife and Claire lying on the floor, stabbed in the heart. Mary screamed, and Edward replied,

'she heard a struggle and a scream'

'She is dead, and there is the knife I did it with. I finished her.' He seemed keen to administer a similar assault on an imaginary male downstairs.

Mary ran to the police, 'with frightened face and wringing her hands'. The police collected tufts of Claire's hair in the kitchen, where he had ripped it out, and they found Edward lying on top of Claire, holding her and kissing her. 'It was an awful spectacle.' He had to be dragged away. He seemed dazed, seemingly unaware of the seriousness of what he had done. 'I will pay anything. I will pay the doctor's fees,' was all he could say, repeatedly.

By the morning he appeared to have gained some understanding of what he had done.

'It is all through jealousy. I should never have done it otherwise. If any man even looked at her, I was jealous.'

Everyone felt that he was unstable; that he needed help. Neighbours reported how he would walk up and down the Strand, glaring at everybody and shaking his head in a strange way. He used a torch to check for men beneath their bed.

Claire was obviously alarmed. She had taken to wearing a kind of body armour – a thick cloth cap as a chest protector. His blade found its way between it and her corset.

Claire was buried in the Ducable family grave in Llanelli. Hyacinthe May and Percy were taken away by her family to live in Newport.

Edward cried bitterly throughout his trial, the *Cambrian* telling us that his sobs 'resounded through the silent court'. He held a white handkerchief before his eyes and gripped the rail of the dock until his knuckles turned white. People were moved by his grief.

The defence claimed it was not murder but manslaughter – a sudden impulse, a temporary insanity, without provocation. Why use a penknife if murder had been his intent? It was the cruellest chance that he had managed to kill her with it.

The jury retired for seventeen minutes and returned a verdict of guilty of manslaughter, which inspired some muted applause in the court. He was sentenced to penal servitude for fifteen years.

CASE NINETEEN 1899

THE PRICE OF IMMORALITY

Suspect: Henry Pelican
Age: Thirty
Charge: Murder

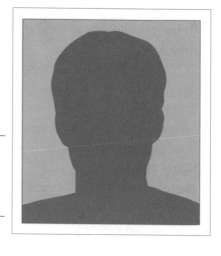

(www.fromoldbooks.org)

You see, as far as I am concerned, a robustly defined customer complaints procedure can prevent any number of problems from getting out of hand. If you need to be convinced, then perhaps you might like to consider the story of Henry Pelican.

What I find so fascinating about this story, and what *The Western Mail* was so eager to describe as a 'squalid murder at Swansea', is the window it opens upon a kind of life in the nineteenth century. The paper claims (though not entirely accurately) that every murder in Swansea had occurred within a radius of a few hundred yards of the address 'the murder circle'. Nonetheless, it was in one of the least favoured parts of the town. It occurred in Baptist Court, 'one of the narrowest and dirtiest alleys in Swansea, a shocking and gruesome tragedy amongst the lowest type of life,'according to the *Cambrian*.

Baptist Court emerged into High Street a few doors above the Bird in Hand Hotel. It overlooked the North Dock, and 'ought to belong to a vanished order of the world', according to the *Cambrian* newspaper. It was at the time next to the Mutoscope exhibition. These were coin-operated 'What the Butler Saw' peep show machines. I don't suppose even the most hardened of butlers would have enjoyed what took place that night.

It happened in the early hours, between 1 and 2 a.m., on Friday 9 June 1899.

A German seaman, Henry Pelican, went with Ellen Waltham (or Sullivan) for an essentially simple and uncomplicated transaction at 1 Baptist Court. The house was kept by William Kingdom and Margaret Tobin, known to the police as 'Sawdust'. Tobin was in prison awaiting trial, and as a consequence, Billy had decided that Ellen was the woman he wanted to share his life with, for a while anyway.

Henry gave Ellen a sovereign, in anticipation of personal services, and, like canny consumers everywhere, he waited for his change.

Ellen, however, seemed to suggest that there were currently no introductory offers available. There was a row and Ellen fled upstairs, seeking the protection of William Kingdom. Henry chased after her, and, she claimed, stabbed her superficially in the abdomen. When William came to her assistance Henry stabbed him twice in the heart, driving the knife in up to the hilt, killing him. He fell down the stairs.

Ellen smashed the windows in an attempt to call for help. Her screams attracted the attentions of PC Hawkins, who found Pelican ready to defend himself. He did, however, surrender himself to the policeman, saying that he had acted in self-defence. They had grabbed him by the neck, 'so that the darkness came before his eyes'.

The press enjoyed the whole thing very much, reflecting upon a sordid story of vice and poverty. Ellen's initial suggestion that the two men were rivals for her affections and had fought for her love was quickly dismissed. The *Western Mail* gleefully indicates that 'There was no sentiment of any kind in the matter'. Those who lived at 1 Baptist Court were 'extremely bad characters'. When Sawdust had been imprisoned, William had brought Ellen in as an alternative. Ellen was generally on the prowl, 'picking up strange seamen'. She had met Henry on Thursday night whilst he was drinking on Wine Street, and then 'decoyed him' to High Street.

What can I tell you about Henry Pelican? He was about thirty years old. He was 'quiet and inoffensive, a well-behaved Prussian'. Praise indeed. In fact he appeared 'more English than German', which must have been a source of some comfort amongst all the difficulties in which he found

'extremely bad characters'

himself. 'There were no traces of brutality or bloodthirstiness in his features.' He was working on the ship *Ravensheugh* and he was regarded as 'decent and a willing worker', though perhaps 'a little weak in the head'. In fact, *The Western Mail* was eager to point out that when his ship had been docked in Cardiff he had drunk nothing else other than ginger beer. But he had all too quickly adopted Swansea habits.

He had arrived two days earlier from Antwerp and started out that Thursday night drinking with his friend Harry, but they had had a fight in the bar of the Coliseum and had been thrown out. This was when Ellen took him home, just before midnight.

The house was a miserable tenement with one room downstairs and one upstairs. There was a small square table, a couple of chairs and a low bed. The table was laid with bread and pickles, suggesting perhaps a jolly midnight feast. By the time Henry Pelican had finished the stairs were covered in blood, for he had with him 'a keen and formidable seaman's knife'.

The neighbours had quite liked Sawdust but found Ellen a bit cheap, to be frank. Kingdom was a muscular dock labourer aged forty-three, but they described him as 'poor Billy', for they knew he was out of his depth with Ellen.

TERRIBLE
MURDER AT SWANSEA.

LABOURER KILLED AND HIS PARAMOUR WOUNDED.

STATEMENT BY THE ASSAILANT.

Shortly after we went to press last Friday morning—and as we briefly announced in a second edition—a terrible murder was committed in Baptist-court, High-street. The victim was a dock labourer named Wm. Kingdom, who lived with a woman of ill-fame, Margaret Tobin, bearing the soubriquet "Sawdust," at No. 1, Baptist-court. The antagonist was a Prussian seaman, Henry Pelican, who has traded for some years to and from South Wales ports, where, amongst a class of acquaintances, he appears to be held in some degree of estimation as a quiet, respectable, and generally-sober individual. There is another victim of Friday's tragedy, a woman by the name of Ellen Waltham, *alias* Sullivan, with whom the fracas which ended so fatally commenced. She, too, was stabbed with the same knife that killed her paramour, and she now lies at the Swansea Hospital in a critical, but not hopeless, condition.

As the nauseating details of the tragedy were unfolded it became evident that it was the outcome of the vice and the sordid conditions of society which arise only too naturally in such a vicinity as that of Baptist-

(By kind permission of SWW Media)

Her arrival as his paramour had not been welcomed by the neighbours. Ellen had met Billy a week before and moved in with him. According to Ellen, he wanted to keep her. After all, he told her that he worked hard and had plenty of money. And to be fair, she said they had been together once before, when she had been in service at the Nag's Head. In the course of their first week together she repeatedly brought men to the house, evidently with Billy's consent.

The National Seaman's and Fireman's Union (now a part of the National Union of Rail, Maritime and Transport Workers) arranged Henry's defences, and in court Ellen's character was skewered. She didn't have a chance. She had appeared before the magistrates on a number of occasions. She had recently been charged with 'pummelling a sailor in the street'. And Henry had asked for change?

She was allegedly twenty-eight, and claimed to have been married for seven years to a man named Waltham, who was currently in the asylum in Gloucester. In fact, Ellen had been an inmate too. She had been originally admitted at the age of nine. Her mother commented that 'she had always had trouble with her head'.

The precise details of the events at the house will never be known. Ellen said that Billy went out to buy whisky for Henry, and that there had been an argument about change. But she also acknowledged that the argument became most heated when they were sitting side by side on the bed. She was asked in court, 'Were you getting your living by immorality?'

She denied it of course, but no one believed her, especially when she admitted that 'a sovereign was the price of immorality'. Her claim that Billy didn't know what was going on was unconvincing. He usually slept downstairs, but on this occasion he went upstairs. When he died he was fully clothed and was even wearing his boots. Perhaps he hadn't expected to be upstairs for too long.

Henry Pelican claimed that he had acted to defend himself, that he had no alternative: 'If they are going to stretch my neck for these two bastards, well I am satisfied.'

But he had no reason to worry. Ellen's past and her profession meant that she had no credibility.

Ellen had been convicted on a previous twenty-seven occasions for assault, drunkenness and prostitution. She had spent time in prison (for robbery and also for wounding) as well as the asylum. She had once promised the court that, 'I'll be different after this. This will be a warning.' But no one was inclined to believe her.

The jury withdrew for about thirty minutes to consider their verdict.

Henry Pelican was acquitted. On 5 August 1899 he set sail once again, thanking the Union for the support they had given him as he left.

CASE TWENTY 1906

I'LL KEEP HOLDING ON

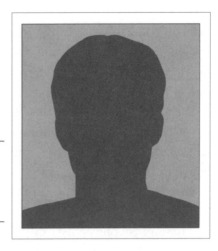

Suspect: William Mitchell
Age: Twenty-four
Charge: Murder

They queued to get into court; to drink up the salacious details of William Mitchell's meeting with Eliza Keast, and to stare at a man whose life was in the balance. Once in the dock, he 'showed signs of acute mental strain' as he pleaded not guilty to murder.

Mitchell was a twenty-four-year-old collier from Deptford who had moved to Abercrave. He was described as having 'an imperfect education', and was only 5ft 2in tall, which was an advantage for a miner. He had come down to Swansea for the weekend, staying in Vaughan's Lodging House.

He had started drinking at 9 a.m. on Saturday 12 May 1906 and had taken a late breakfast in the early afternoon. He drank about eight pints of beer during the day, though he had taken some time off to buy a pair of trousers for 4s 6d. He was steadily working his way through the 17s he had brought with him for the weekend. By the evening he only had a few scraps of change left.

Eliza, the daughter of respectable parents, was described as having followed a 'base and immoral life'. *The Cambrian* described her death as 'A Wayward Daughter's End'. Her father was a labourer at the Hafod Copperworks, and the family

Eliza Keast. (Original illustration by Angela Warne-Payne, based on a contemporary sketch)

lived at 102 Pentre Treharne Road. Eliza had moved out to Vaughan's Lodging House on the Strand, where she was drinking heavily. She had previous convictions for indecency, though she 'was singularly quiet for one of her class when sober'.

The prosecution stressed that the case was not based upon circumstantial evidence, but upon eyewitness accounts. But the eyewitnesses only saw small parts of the awful events, and crucially, no one really saw the order in which things happened.

They had met at 10 p.m., on the Strand.

'Hello ducky,' she said. 'Give me a match.'

'I haven't got one on me, my old darling.'

Ah yes. The language of love.

Patrick Long, seventeen, saw them meet at the bottom of Green Dragon Lane. He heard Mitchell make a suggestion to Keast, and then they started bargaining.

She said, 'Come down this way,' and they went into Padley's Yard together. It was, as they said in court, 'a place often used for immoral purposes'. They seemed to be drunk. Shortly afterwards, Long happened to peer through the crack of a door in Gough's Lodging House, which backed onto the yard. He saw Mitchell apparently sitting on top of Eliza. He had his left hand round her throat and was striking her with his right. Long could hear a gurgling noise. He rushed around and raised the alarm. He shouted out, 'Let the woman alone!'

Having no effect at all, he went off for help and came back with a woman called Kate Hughes. They found the couple lying quite still. Kate thought they were both dead. Suddenly Mitchell jumped up and ran, knocking Kate over the shafts of a cart.

A man called Yates pursued Mitchell, and there was a fight. Mitchell was dragged back to the scene, where he was 'roughly treated' by a number of bystanders. Mitchell was pinned against the wall whilst they waited for the police to arrive. He cried out, 'Let me go at her again!'

He seemed to be rather angry. He did calm down though, when he was told that Eliza was dead.

'I am to blame,' he said. 'I suppose I shall swing for it.' He also said that the crowd around him were so hostile, that if the police hadn't turned up 'I would have been dead too.'

The Keast family lived here, on Pentre Treharne Road. (Author's collection)

Mitchell had strangled Eliza. Her face was congested and her ears and nose were blue. There were fingernail marks on her throat, wrist and arm. Her tongue was swollen and coated in dirt. Her dress was drawn untidily up to her waist. There was a shilling coin beneath her body. It was hard to anticipate what Mitchell could say. But his defence was unusual and unexpected.

When he gave his evidence, he said that they had agreed on a fee of 2s for the service she was prepared to offer. They went into Padley's Yard behind a wagon, where it was very dark.

Eliza had asked for the money, but when he looked in his pocket he only had 1s. He offered it to her, and 'seeing that she made no objections, he began'.

Then she started to shout. 'No you don't, you bastard!'

She started to hit him, and grabbed and crushed his sensitive equipment. 'After this act by the deceased, he hardly knew what had happened.' Well, it is a particularly sensitive area.

He lashed out and may have grabbed her by the throat and by the arm, but he couldn't remember. He struggled to pull away, but her grip was fierce and he was in tremendous pain. In the end he stopped struggling and slumped on top of Eliza because he felt so weak and helpless. He didn't think he had done anything. All he could think of was his once-vibrant and now injured manhood, which Eliza had crushed in a vice-like grip for what felt like hours.

'There were fingernail marks on her throat, wrist and arm'

He had little recollection of anything else. The running away, the fight, the baying crowd. None of it, he said, he could recall.

The defence counsel said 'he had tasted well-nigh the taste of death. He would be forever haunted by his crime'.

'The thought would be with him in the dark watches of the night, and would present itself in the hour of his greatest enjoyment.'

He was obviously fighting for his life, but Eliza had lost that fight some time ago and there was no one there to speak for her. The prosecution said all this was an invention. He hadn't mentioned it before, and had spent all his time working out a ridiculous story.

But in his summing-up, the judge, Mr Justice Jelf, clearly sided with Mitchell. In a speech which must have brought tears to the eyes of an all-male jury, he reflected upon the vulnerability of the male body. The pain Mitchell experienced would have been known to them from their time playing sports when they 'had been kicked or perhaps struck by a cricket ball'. In such circumstances it is not a surprise that he became unconscious of his actions.

When he had finished, the jury were effectively stitched up. They went out for half an hour and returned a verdict of guilty of manslaughter, with a strong recommendation to mercy.

Justice Jelf agreed with the verdict. Mitchell had gone far beyond what was required for self-defence but he had been provoked. So it was six months' imprisonment with hard labour.

There was some applause in the gallery, though most people were surprised. They felt he had been extremely lucky. Certainly you can't help thinking that a female jury would have been less sympathetic. After all, there was no one to refute his version of events. And perhaps, in the end, that is the point. The order of events was always crucial. What was grabbed first? The jewels? Or the throat? Because that fact makes an enormous difference. Who was actually acting in self-defence?

But no matter how thrilled some may have been by the details of a sordid crime in sordid circumstances, no one should lose sight of the tragedy. A young woman, trapped by drink and lifestyle, had died at the hands of a stranger in a cold dark yard – the final triumph of the life she had adopted.

CASE TWENTY-ONE   1919

'I THOUGHT YOU WAS A POLICEMAN'

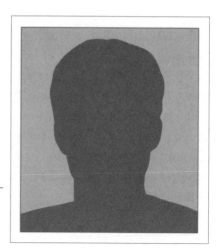

Suspect:	George Shotton
Age:	Thirty-nine
Charge:	Bigamy

Swansea's history starts with the discovery of bones in a cave in Gower – The Red Lady of Paviland, the first human fossil ever found. Incomplete perhaps, and it was a male skeleton not a female one, but significant nonetheless. However, there was also another discovery in a cave, a little nearer Swansea. There were more bones this time, a full skeleton, and they were undeniably those of a woman. Because these were the haunted bones of Mamie Stuart, murdered in Caswell in November 1919.

Poor Mamie. A simple girl really. A girl of uncomplicated pleasures. A show girl; a singer, dancer and pianist. She came from Sunderland and was regarded

Mamie Stuart. (By kind permission of SWW Media)

as attractive, despite faint scars on her face from an attack by a dog when she was a child. She was originally part of a popular theatrical troupe called 'The Five Verona Girls'. However, one broke her ankle and another became pregnant, so they were five no more. At this point it appears that she met George Shotton, probably in South Shields in 1917. He was a marine surveyor, which involved checking out ships and travelling all over the country. He told Mamie that he was a widower who lived in Swansea, and subsequently she wrote to him at the Grosvenor Hotel there. Soon they were living together, and they married in Sunderland in March 1918. They honeymooned in Droitwich Spa, which just goes to show that the spark of true romance illuminated their lives. Then it was back to real life in Bayswater in Bristol and then Trafalgar Terrace in Swansea, which today forms part of Oystermouth Road, where they lodged with Mrs Hearns.

But there was a problem. Mamie believed quite rightly that she was married to George. She had a certificate and everything. But George was a bigamist. For reasons best known to himself, George Shotton had chosen to seriously over-complicate his life. You see, he was already married to Mary. They had in fact been married since 1905. They had a son, George Rex, and they lived in Penarth.

Now you might imagine that George wanted to keep these two relationships entirely separate. His scheme involved keeping Mamie alone at home, ever ready to provide him with rest and relaxation. Except Mamie was not that kind of girl. For her, it was profoundly boring. She told Mrs Hearns of her desire to return to the stage, and there were numerous arguments. George was not happy with her shopping trips to Swansea, and neither was he too keen on what you might describe as her flirtations.

His time with Mamie was certainly volatile.

At one point she saw George with his family in Mumbles, and retreated to her parents in Sunderland. For whatever reason they were reconciled, and she returned to Swansea to a house called Ty Llonydd in Newton. Shortly afterwards, at the end of 1919, she disappeared. There was always the possibility that she had gone off back to London, but no one knew for certain.

Her disappearance was not reported until May 1920, when her sister wrote to Mrs Hearns asking her to find Mamie. This made Mrs Hearns remember something that Mamie had once said: 'If I am ever missing, do your very utmost to find me.'

Now why should she say that?

Soon the police became involved. George, Mary and George Rex were now living in Caswell. Shotton admitted to having had a relationship with Mamie, but said she had claimed to have found someone who could take better care of her than he could, and had walked out. Of course once the police began to take an interest, the bigamous nature of their marriage was quickly exposed.

George was charged with bigamy and appeared in court in May 1920. He claimed that he had been impersonated at the ceremony in Sunderland. It wasn't him at all. However, Mamie's sister indicated that George frequently referred to Mamie as 'my own little wife', and used other moving terms of endearment. He signed letters with 'your loving husband', and this led the police to an inescapable conclusion. You couldn't really blame them.

At the same time, a leather trunk was found at the Grosvenor Hotel containing items belonging to Mamie, including dresses which had been slashed to pieces.

George was found guilty of bigamy and imprisoned for eighteen months. Mary divorced him and the police started to dig up the garden. It was pretty clear what had happened, but, try as they might, the police could find no forensic evidence. No body, no crime. It was suggested that she might have been seen on a boat to Canada, disappearing with her lover. As a conclusion to a perplexing story, this was as good as any.

And so the case remained for forty years. George served his time and took on a range of jobs – an odd job man in a nursing home, a motor mechanic. Eventually he ended up in an old people's home in 1947 in Bristol. He was a regular churchgoer and died of a stroke in 1958 at the age of seventy-eight.

And all that time he carried with him a terrible secret. He must have had horrible images in his mind.

We can speculate on why Mamie was killed. She was happy to talk about her other liaisons to him – after all, he had betrayed her first. But perhaps whilst he celebrated his own sexual freedom, he could not accept Mamie's. He needed to control her, but she was not the kind of girl who could ever be

'he carried with him a terrible secret'

controlled. It is possible to speculate how he did it, but we will never know. By the time she was discovered, all her soft tissue had long gone.

But of course, however he killed her, Shotton had the problem of dealing with the body. He solved it by cutting it up. We know this from the marks on her bones where the saw failed to grip. The memory of this must have been always in his mind. He cut her body into three sections and then stuffed

Disappearance of woman in 1919

By " EVENING POST " REPORTER

DISCOVERY OF A SKELETON IN A BRANDY COVE MINE-SHAFT CAVITY YESTERDAY, BY THREE YOUNG BISHOP-STON MEN WHO WERE CAVE-EXPLORING, GIVES RISE TO THE QUESTION : " ARE THESE THE REMAINS OF MAMIE STUART ? "

The 26-year-old brunette was missed in 1919. She had been living with a man who had married her bigamously, and police up and down the country made a vain search for any clue as to her whereabouts.

It was at Swansea that Mamie's belongings were discovered in a portmanteau. Her jewellery was there, but not the broad gold band wedding ring she had worn after her " marriage " nor the three-stone engagement ring which had been given her.

Mamie Stuart was known to have an eye tooth missing, and police did not deny today that an eye tooth was missing from the skull found yesterday.

They made no comment, either, on the suggestion that there was a mark on the side of the skull which could have been from a dog bite — which Mamie Stuart had suffered during her short life.

POLICE OFFICERS investi-gate the air-shaft on the cliff between Brandy Cove and Caswell Bay where a skeleton, believed to be that of a woman, was found yesterday. Investigations are being carried out by Detective-Chief Superintendent T. J. Williams. With him are Detective Inspector G. R. Williams, Cowerton, Detective-Sergeant Reuben Davies, Sergeant W. Davies and Constable Barnett, of Bishopston. Picture on left shows the three pot-holers who found the skeleton. Left to right, Colin McNamara, John Gerke, and Graham Jones.

(By kind permission of SWW Media)

them into a sack. He took her to a mineshaft in Brandy Cove and dumped her there.

And so Mamie came to haunt Brandy Cove. Apparently a couple on a romantic walk along the lonely path heard the shrieks of a woman, which seemed to come from below their feet. Brandy Cove was soon regarded as being seriously haunted. A man fishing from the rocks heard her too, but could find nothing. George had hidden the body well. And Mamie stayed hidden for a long time, for over forty years.

In November 1961, three young men from Bishopston, led by John Gerke, went down the air shaft of an old lead mine at Brandy Cove and crawled into a narrow opening. Behind a rock they found a pile of bones. Picking up a sheep's rib, Gerke slipped it into an eye socket and lifted up a human skull.

The police were called, but unfortunately the officers were too generously proportioned to get into the cave themselves, so the three cavers recovered the bones. They found a complete skeleton,

(By kind permission of SWW Media)

a rotting sack in which the bones had once been contained, some jewellery and a clip with hair still tangled in it.

It was pretty obvious who they had found. Everything quickly fell into place. Poor Mamie. After all these years. And it wasn't suicide. Dead people rarely cut themselves up with saws.

At the inquest in Gowerton, an interesting detail emerged. William Symons, by now eighty-three, had been the postman in Newton at the time of Mamie's death. Whilst out on delivery, he had seen George struggling to his yellow van with a large and heavy sack. William had offered to give him a hand, and George had jumped, saying, 'Oh God, I thought you was a policeman.' He declined the kind offer, and once loaded, drove off towards Brandy Cove.

It never occurred to William that this might have been important.

CASE TWENTY-TWO   1929

COLD FISH

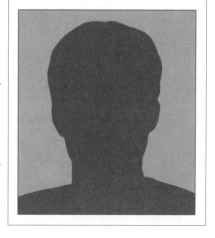

Suspect: Thomas Jackson
Age: Thirty-nine
Charge: Murder

It remains a strange, haunting tale, littered with lies and fantasy, which reached a terrible conclusion in a brutal murder in Mumbles. As we try to untangle this mess, please remember that Ethel M. Dell wrote a novel

MRS. JACKSON DIES IN SWANSEA HOSPITAL.

Sensational Bungalow Crime May Remain an Unsolved Mystery.

MADAME "X" CARRIES HER SECRET TO THE GRAVE.

Mrs. Kate Jackson, the victim of the Limeslade bungalow attack, late on the night of Monday of last week, died in Swansea Hospital at midday on Sunday. During her periods of semi-consciousness, in the intervening days, she only muttered vague and meaningless phrases, and the secret of the identity of her assailant, or assailants, has apparently been carried with her to the grave.

At the moment it would appear that the murder of Madame "X"—for the police are apparently satisfied that it was a murder—must remain one of the famous unsolved problems in the annals of British crime.

From the time of the tragic happening the Swansea police have been engaged in the most active inquiries, but without the aid of a statement from the woman, who is now dead, they were well-nigh hopelessly handicapped from the beginning. Anyhow, this much is definitely true, that no arrest is immediately imminent, and any suspicions the police may entertain they are naturally keeping to themselves.

If the life story of Madame "X" should be fully revealed, it is understood that she will prove to have been a clever adventuress of infinite daring.

(By kind permission of SWW Media)

called *The Bars of Iron*, and that Kate Jackson was beaten to death with a tyre lever in February 1929. And that her husband Thomas Jackson got away with it.

After her murder, Thomas was questioned by the police.

He told them that it had all started in 1919 on the Strand in London, when he met Molly, who claimed to be the common-law wife of a French artist called Leopold le Grys. She also said she was the youngest daughter of Lord Abercorn and a novelist too, writing under the name of Ethel M. Dell.

He had believed it all. When they married in Camberwell in 1920, Molly persuaded him to use the title Captain Gordon Ingram, since it sounded sophisticated. She had a 'peculiar vanity' he said, and he was eager to please her. Under this name they lived in Farnborough.

This deceit, however, unsettled Thomas and he insisted in 1922 that they went through the marriage a second time, using proper names. Molly's birth certificate indicated that she was in fact Katherine Atkinson from the North East of England. Molly laughed. This was merely an identity she had bought in 1916 from a girl who went to live in Australia. They married again in Cardiff in September 1922 and lived together at The Laurels, a bungalow in Mumbles.

Thomas was increasingly unsettled by Kate. She insisted on being called Molly and was angry when he called her Kate. There was obviously so much that he didn't know about her. He felt she wanted him to protect her, though she never said from whom.

Her lifestyle was recklessly extravagant. She dressed only in silk and had no sense of value. He told officers that she kept a revolver and ammunition, to protect herself against kidnappers. She would make unexplained visits to London. And then in 1927 she was called to give evidence in the case of George William Harrison, who was accused of embezzling almost £20,000 from union funds under his control.

Harrison had been the Secretary of the National Association of Coopers. In 1927 he was sentenced to five years' imprisonment for embezzling £19,000 from the Association, leaving them with only £3 1s 10d. He had given at least £8,000 to a woman he believed was Molly le Grys, who, as we

'Her lifestyle was recklessly extravagant'

have seen, was Kate Jackson. They had met in 1914 when he was thirty-nine. She had told him that she was a woman of good position, whose parents had disinherited her.

Harrison never really profited from the money he stole. He gave it to Kate because she claimed she needed it for medical attention. He had forged receipts for the money, some of which had been raised by a levy of 1s a week in aid of the Miners' Relief Fund during the General Strike. They should have received about £700, but didn't.

At Harrison's trial at the Old Bailey, Kate was referred to as 'Madame X', her name withheld in the hope that she would return some of the money.

It certainly fuelled sensational headlines in the press and added to the aura which surrounded her. Sub-editors described the missing money as 'Money for Miners', and such words would come back to haunt her, because when she had appeared at the remand hearing in March 1927, she gave evidence in her own name. She confirmed she had received £8,000 or so, which she had used to buy The Laurels. She denied that he sent her sums like £25 or £40 per week. It was more like £15 or £20. But however much it was, it wasn't his money. Other people felt it was right-fully theirs. Why did he send the money? The press had their own opinions and, no doubt, so did their readers. But Harrison was in prison, she was in Mumbles, and some people were in a very agitated state of mind.

The Jacksons moved to a bungalow called Kenilworth in Plunch Lane, Limeslade in 1928. They adopted a young girl called Betty, who Kate claimed was the illegitimate daughter of Baron Willoughby de Broke. It was apparently her duty to shelter her from a vengeful family.

On 10 February 1929 Kate went to the cinema with her next-door neigh-bour, Olive Dimmock. Thomas was babysitting. They returned home at 10 p.m. It was cold, dark and damp. Olive said goodnight, and Kate walked to her home, which was clearly lit.

Suddenly, Olive heard screams. She ran round to the back of Kenilworth and found Thomas kneeling over Kate, who was lying on the ground. She saw no one else.

Kate was helped inside. She had severe head wounds. There were nine separate injuries to her scalp, and other bruises to her arms and shoul-ders. Her fingernail had been torn off. Thomas did not send for a doctor immediately, believing, he said, that she would recover. When the doctor was called two hours after the attack, she was immediately admitted to hospital. She was repeatedly asked: 'Who has done this?'

All she ever said in reply in her semi-conscious state was 'Gorse'. No one knew what she meant. She never made a statement. She died six days later of heart failure, following a fractured skull and brain haemorrhage.

Thomas Jackson was arrested. His failure to tell the police about the assault immediately was felt to be suspicious. Also, under a cushion in the house, they found a tyre lever, which they believed was the murder weapon. He admitted he had a tyre lever, but said that it was in his tool box. He had no idea how another tyre lever had found its way underneath a cushion. Perhaps Kate had put it there. And anyway, he said, there was a glass flagon missing from outside. Perhaps that was used to beat her, not a tyre lever. The bloodstains on his clothes had got there when he had been helping her.

There was so much that the police found hard to believe. Little he said made any sense at all. He said that they had a warm and loving relationship. They had been married for nine years, but he had no idea who she was. Every Wednesday she would receive money through the post which, she claimed, were royalties for her writing. She had also received threatening letters, which he felt were connected with the Harrison trial. Perhaps the money she received related to this as well.

Thomas said he had been a Captain in the war, and had been wounded. He had gone to London for some rest and recuperation in 1919, and had visited Lyons Coffee House on the Strand. He had ordered a piece of cold fish, and an attractive woman had approached him and said he resembled a friend of hers called Lord Carroll. Of course it was Kate, though she introduced herself as Molly le Grys. She told him that he looked 'too ill to eat such a poor meal' and immediately ordered more expensive food.

As their relationship developed, he began to believe that she was highly educated and had mixed in the highest social circles. He said she spoke

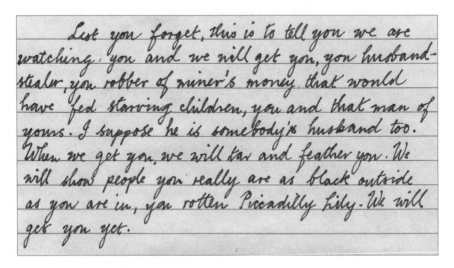

Lest you forget, this is to tell you we are watching you and we will get you, you husband-stealer, you robber of miner's money that would have fed starving children, you and that man of yours. I suppose he is somebody's husband too. When we get you, we will tar and feather you. We will show people you really are as black outside as you are in, you rotten Piccadilly Lily. We will get you yet.

(Original artwork by Gill Figg)

French fluently and was familiar with Russian, Dutch and Italian. She had been educated in Brussels and had run away with le Grys, a French portrait painter. She bought French novels and spent long hours in bed, either reading or writing, since she was under contract as a journalist to London newspapers. Kate would post letters to Mr Carter at the Minories in London. She said he was the Head of the Secret Police for whom she was working (though it was in fact William Harrison).

According to Thomas, she seemed to live her life in terror and often had fainting fits, a consequence of nervous strain. If she heard a car she would switch the lights off and hide, fearing that agents were coming to reclaim Betty. The threatening letters she received made her live life on edge.

The police were not convinced by any of this and quickly dismantled Jackson's illusions – or delusions. When faced with such a bewildering and unexpected set of circumstances, the police brought a brutal common sense to the whole thing. And they were pretty certain they had got their man. Generally speaking, and without wishing to make assumptions about anyone's domestic arrangements, tyre levers are rarely stored for ease of access beneath cushions in the lounge.

So the police went back to basics and explored Kate's life story in close detail.

She was born in Wray in Lancashire in 1885. Her parents were John and Agnes Atkinson. They identified her through a deformed thumbnail, since she had trapped her thumb in a mangle as a child. She wasn't a writer at all; she could neither read nor speak a word of any continental language.

The police started to ask themselves: who had invented all this? Was it in fact Thomas Jackson, not Kate at all?

His behaviour was also odd. He hadn't called for help straightaway when Kate was assaulted, and when he met the doctor some distance from the house, he talked about bad roads and poor lighting and about the rates, but not once about his wife.

Jackson was tried for murder at the Glamorgan Summer Assizes in 1929.

The prosecution said he had concocted this elaborate fantasy himself. Thomas could not afford Kate's extravagant habits, and he wanted her out of the way. She had paid her way initially, but when the Harrison money dried up, he couldn't support her. He was as big a liar as his wife. He had probably written the anonymous letters himself. Keep it simple. This was no contract killing.

The defence? Well he was devoted to her. They had never had a cross word.

Robert Atkinson, Kate's brother and a Liverpool fireman, appeared in court. He said, 'On behalf of the family, we go out to my brother-in-law with open arms and love.'

They certainly didn't think he had done it. And the letters? They were genuine, and suggested that she had been blackmailing someone about the Harrison case. Someone with a grudge had come looking for her.

The summing-up by the judge was not sympathetic. 'There is no evidence of any secret enemy; that is merely a surmise or possibility.'

The jury were equally certain. They were far more entranced by the excitement and the mystery of it all than the judge had been. They were out for just half an hour. A not guilty verdict was returned. The gallery cheered and clapped. On hearing this, people outside the court cheered too. The crowd was so dense that the traffic outside the Guildhall ground to a halt. Jackson was hugged and kissed by women, and men played on banjos and mandolins.

On his return to Mumbles, Jackson was cheered by crowds outside the bungalow. He sold his story to the *Empire News*. A waxworks exhibition in Weston-super-Mare wrote to the newspapers asking for photographs, so that they could make models of the main characters.

But the police never looked for anyone else in connection with Kate's death. They knew that Thomas had done it. They regarded him as a man of 'low moral character'. He was 'evasive and unconcerned'. The basis for their certainty is clearly displayed in the records of the police investigation, held in the National Archives in Kew and closed from public view for seventy-five years. These files give a completely different picture of the case. For if Kate was a fantasist, then Thomas was a liar.

Thomas Jackson

Thomas Jackson was born in 1890 in Foxhole in Swansea, where his father, Thomas Henry, ran the Ship Inn. He had worked as a coal-tip man in Swansea Docks before he enlisted in the army on 9 August 1912. He served for two months in France at the beginning of the First World War and had been wounded at Ypres. He was then sent to India for ten months. In total he served for three years and 265 days, and never progressed beyond the rank of private. He was discharged in April 1916 with a pension of 12s 6d per week. He lived for a while at 70 Alexandra Terrace, Brynmill, with a prostitute called May Jones, whom he supported with his earnings as a billiard player. They moved to lodgings in Landore, where there was a woman called Martha Ingram who was married to an actor. In the early part of 1919 he stole her marriage certificate and went to London, where he stayed at the YMCA in Camberwell. On 11 January he received £162 for commuting his pension and indicated that he was going to emigrate to Rhodesia. Then he met Kate.

Kate Atkinson

She was born in 1887 and ran away from home in search of a career on the stage, perhaps in 1903. Soon she was working as a prostitute.

Kate meets Leopold le Grys

When the police found Leopold le Grys, he was running a hotel at 3 Eastbourne Terrace, Paddington, with his wife and his son Leslie (born in 1902) from his first marriage to Charlotte, who had died.

He had first met Kate in Piccadilly in 1910, when she had introduced herself as Lady Mary Hamilton. She said she worked as society reporter for *The Times*. Soon they were living together in Kings Cross. She would obtain manuscripts for him to illustrate. When they were complete she would tell publishers that she had done them, and indeed Leopold did sign them as 'Madame le Grys'. Then, in 1915, Kate unexpectedly went off to Bournemouth. He followed her there and then was called up to serve in the Army Veterinary Corps, with whom he remained for the duration of the war. Kate looked after Leslie, for which le Grys gave her a small allowance. In 1918 she sent Leslie to his father in Aldershot, saying that she would not keep him any more. Leslie got a job as a taxi driver and le Grys found a room in Aldershot. When Leslie asked for the return of his record collection from Kate in 1919, Leopold went to collect it and was assaulted by Jackson, who struck him in the face and on the jaw.

Leopold confirmed that Kate was neither a writer nor an artist; she couldn't speak French or indeed any other language. 'She was uneducated but of very plausible personality.'

Kate meets William Harrison

Whilst she was still living with le Grys, Kate met William Harrison. He made his statement in Maidstone Prison where he was serving his five-year stretch. He met her on Charing Cross Road in September 1914. There had been a slight motor accident, and Kate, on seeing it, appeared to faint. Harrison assisted her, and she told him that she had not eaten for three days. At her suggestion, he took her to a restaurant in Wardour Street, where they ate. Later that afternoon they had sex for the first time.

She told him that her name was Madame le Grys, daughter of nobility, widow and mother of a son called Leslie. Soon they were meeting weekly, and according to Harrison had sex on two or three occasions. In March 1915 she announced that she was pregnant and needed money for a termination. He paid her £40. Then he had a letter from a Mrs Humber of Bournemouth (though of course this was Kate herself), saying that urgent life-saving medical attention was required. Her disappearance to Bournemouth was supported by le Grys, as we have seen. Harrison then sent her between £20 and £30 each week until he was arrested in 1927.

Kate meets Thomas

There is no doubt that she was working as a prostitute when Thomas met her in 1919, and they married very soon after that meeting. How many of her stories Thomas believed we will never know, but he was as unreliable as her. It seems clear that the idea of getting married in the name of Ingram must have come from the stolen marriage certificate. Their marriage certificate from Camberwell on 24 March 1919 makes interesting reading. Thomas gives his name as Gordon Ingram from East Dulwich and gives his occupation as Music Hall Artist and his father's as a journalist. Such ideas were clearly lifted from that stolen document.

Their life together

They lived initially in Farnborough, where Thomas was well known as a billiard player. He made little financial contribution to their life together. They were living off Harrison's money, as they did right up to the moment he was arrested in 1927.

They moved to Warwick Farm in Ash, Surrey, for a while. There Kate had a relationship with a poultry dealer called Willis. As a result, his wife applied for a separation order. In a temporary reconciliation, Willis told his wife that it had all started because Mrs Ingram owed him money. Throughout her life Kate had only one currency she could rely on, and she was happy to use that regularly. She told Olive Dimmock that whilst they were there, Thomas once tried to strangle her. He had also hit her with a broom.

They moved to Swansea when they exchanged the farm for a house at 130 Rhondda Street, and continued to live off the money she received.

Thomas said that she spent most of her time writing novels in the name of Ethel Dell. The real Ethel Dell was a reclusive writer of popular romantic fiction and author of *The Bars of Iron*. Kate certainly did not appear to live in the state of fear that Thomas claimed. She frequently went off alone in the late summer collecting blackberries.

He told the police that they never quarrelled, but in fact their relationship was a tempestuous one. Neighbours heard him say, 'I shall be glad to get rid of her. I hope she will go.' He said he wished that a wave would come and take her out to sea when she was swimming. He said that she beat him, and that she had chased him with a fish filleting knife. She called him 'a bald-headed bugger'. On more than one occasion she threw his clothes into the garden.

For a while they lived apart. In June 1927 Thomas was lodging at 17 Western Street. His landlady, Rhoda Phillips, kicked him out because he spent his days in the doorway whistling at girls. He did nothing except play billiards and keep very late hours. He returned one night with a woman from Cardiff, a milliner, and he asked Rhoda to tell her what she knew about him, as they intended to marry. When she said that he couldn't marry since he already had a wife, he said that it didn't count since Kate already had a husband anyway. Perhaps that is why he had insisted on the second marriage in his own name.

They moved to Limeslade in 1927, when their source of income ceased with Harrison's arrest and they had to surrender The Laurels to the National Union of Coopers. Jackson rented a billiard room, then he worked as a coal merchant and then as a fishmonger but with no success. Something had to change. He couldn't keep her, and she could no longer keep him.

Betty

She was born on 31 December 1922 to Millicent Hawkins, a private secretary in Farnborough, and was named Joyce Daphne.

Olive Dimmock

It is when you consider Mrs Dimmock and the role that she played that everything starts to fall into place, just as it did for the police officers. She is the final piece of the jigsaw. Thomas was on 'particularly familiar terms' with 'Dimmie'. They were well known around Mumbles, and were seen frequently arm in arm. They would go shopping together. Interestingly he called her Molly, and when he was working in the fish market, he employed her son.

A neighbour, Mrs Gammon, said that she once looked through the window and saw Kate and Thomas in bed together with Olive.

After the murder, Mrs Dimmock started to look after Thomas and was rarely out of the house. She was there more often than she was at home. On 19 February, Jackson and Dimmock were seen by the police to enter the bedroom in the bungalow and to close the door. They remained there for half an hour.

Olive was already well known to the police and they were convinced that she was colluding with Thomas to hide evidence. When he went to the hospital with Kate after the attack, Olive lit a fire in the house, which caused a strange smell to fill the street. Was she destroying evidence? Was she burning bloodstained clothes?

The death of Kate Jackson

She hadn't been attacked outside at all. She had been attacked in the scullery, when she was taking her coat off. There was no blood on the collar of her coat, as there would have been if she had been wearing it. The coat was found on the floor in the scullery. There was blood on the bottom, and the police believed either that she had taken it off just before the assault and had used it vainly to protect herself, or it had been used to muffle her cries. There was blood all over the scullery. Thomas suggested she had been attacked with a beer flagon that was outside, but since there was blood on both the inside and outside of the flagon, it must already have been broken before she was attacked. The police believed she had been attacked with

Kate's grave in Llansamlet has been lost. Could this be it? (Author's collection)

the tyre lever and that she had bled onto the broken glass. She had been dragged outside – and since she was a big girl (15 or 16 stone), it must have taken two to do it.

As the judge said, Jackson's behaviour seemed inconsistent with a man whose wife had been attacked and severely injured. The attack was never reported to the police. They only found out about it when they were informed by the hospital.

They were convinced that the anonymous letters had been written by Thomas Jackson. They had been posted in Swansea Central and Morriston.

The police arrested him before they were ready, before they had assembled all the evidence. There was a suggestion that he might drown himself, and so they had to act. But you can see why they knew they had got their man. For them it was enormously frustrating that the jury were seduced by the fantasy woven around the death of a bogus novelist.

The police announced that Kate was to be buried in Danygraig Cemetery. It is fitting, perhaps, that she was in fact buried in Llansamlet.

Sadly, her grave has disappeared into the earth.

SLOW COOKER

Suspect:	Allan Mclean
Age:	Twenty-six
Charge:	Murder

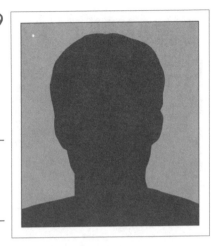

The body was identified by William Richards. He confirmed that it was his mother-in-law, the wife of a labourer called William Webber. She might have been known to some as May Taylor, but her name was Ruth Webber and she was forty-three years old. She was living in a flat at 38 Trafalgar Terrace, on the corner with Beach Street. Her body was found by Mrs Hammond, who took her an early-morning cup of tea on 18 January 1939 and found the room full of smoke. It was not a pretty sight. Her legs and the lower part of her body had been burnt away. An oil lamp, which, it is assumed, must have set fire to the clothes, was overturned on the bed. Death was due to asphyxia and the shock brought on by extensive burns.

It was initially a simple, if gruesome, newspaper report in the *South Wales Daily Post*. But the police started to take an interest right from the start, believing that the fire was just a feeble attempt to destroy evidence. The following week Allan Mclean, a twenty-six-year-old seaman of no fixed abode, was charged with her murder. They believed he had strangled her.

Mclean was a sailor from Greenock in Scotland, and he had been discharged from the *Fidra* on the morning of 17 January 1939. He had gone first to the cinema, and then started drinking in various pubs until he had ended up in the Black Lion.

Ruth Webber had also gone out drinking, with her friend Mrs Olsen. They had been to the Rum Puncheon and made their way to the Black Lion. There they met Mclean. They played darts and they drank. By 9 p.m. they

SWANSEA
FIRE DEATH
MYSTERY

(By kind permission of SWW Media)

were drinking cheap white wine in the Brooklands Hotel. They bought a flagon of beer and took it back to Trafalgar Terrace, where Mamie Stuart once lived.

What happened next is hazy in places, but that reflects the condition of the protagonists in this horrid little tale. Such are the consequences of cheap white wine. We can, though, piece together a version of what probably happened. It would seem that Ruth asked Mclean for 10s, which he promptly handed over. Ruth dimmed the light on the oil lamp and got into bed. He took his clothes off, climbed into bed and immediately fell asleep. He woke suddenly to find himself staring at the wall. He turned over to see Ruth going through his pockets.

Where Ruth died. Picture taken in November 2012. (Author's collection)

He called her a dirty little thief and jumped out of bed. He pushed her over, and she banged her head on the bed frame. He remembered there being blood on her face. She started screaming and swearing, and, fearful that someone would hear, he clamped his hand over her mouth. Then she was lying on the bed, mumbling. He searched for his clothes. He might have used the lamp to find them. He put the bedclothes over her on the bed. He left. It was around midnight and too late to get a room in the Seaman's Home, so he slept in a bus shelter.

Of course, the only one who could offer any explanation of what happened was Mclean, and he obviously tried to present his actions in the best light that he could. He must have shown much more violence and aggression than he admitted in court, as Ruth's injuries indicated. He admitted that he was there, but he denied murder. Whatever happened had been a complete accident. He denied moving the lamp deliberately. If he'd known she was in

'he clamped his hand over her mouth'

danger he would not have left, though you may question whether he knew anything at all.

Ruth wasn't dead when he left. But the oil lamp was amongst the bed linen and had set light to the flock mattress. It had smouldered for about eight hours and Ruth Webber had 'slowly roasted or simply cooked to death'. There was carbon in her windpipe, which showed she had inhaled but was so deeply unconscious that the pain of being burned alive didn't wake her. There were no burns on her hands so she had not tried to bat out the flames.

Two residents, the Lewis brothers, answered Mrs Hammond's screams and carried the body onto the landing, burning their hands in the process. It must have been an awful sight.

The fire had been clearly defined in the centre of the bed. Neither the clothes at the bottom nor the pillows at the top were touched.

According to the *South Wales Daily Post*, 'the lower part of the torso was completely burned, and as far as the legs were concerned, there was nothing but a few bits of bone found amongst the bedding.'

Her head injuries, however, were plain to see. There were extensive bruises on the face, lacerations over the left eye and haemorrhages to each side of the voice box.

Woman Found Dead on Burning Bed

Overturned Lamp Mystery

Members of Swansea C.I.D under Detective-inspector J. Wright on Wednesday investigated the circumstances in which Mrs. Ruth Webber, aged 43, of Trafalgar

(By kind permission of SWW Media)

Does Not Remember What He Did With Lamp

WHEN the hearing was resumed at Glamorgan Assizes to-day of the case in which Allan McLean, a seaman, was charged with the murder of Ruth Webber at Trafalgar-terrace, Swansea, on January 1 McLean entered the witness-box.

McLean said he was 24. He arrived in Swansea on Saturday, January 14, and on the Tuesday he was discharged from his ship.

He described how he saw Ruth in doing so he picked up the lamp. discharge papers and personal belongings were lying on the floor. He found his trousers " sticking " from under

(By kind permission of SWW Media)

The prosecution were convinced that Mclean had used great violence on her. Webber and Mclean had certainly quarrelled and he had certainly been the last person to see her alive. He had hit her on the head with something – perhaps the oil lamp – and then strangled her to unconsciousness. There was an extensive bruise on the right lower jaw which extended down to the bone. She hadn't been hit once, but several times. The question was how did the oil lamp end up on the bed? Was it accidental, a consequence of moving an untidy pile of bedding and clothes? Or had it been a deliberate attempt to destroy her, to cover up the evidence of his attack? The oil lamp had been moved onto the bed. It hadn't got there on its own. Only two people could have done it. And one was dead and one was facing possible hanging.

Mclean had given himself up to the police on the evening of 18 January 1939. He had been in the Commercial Inn in Landore, where he read about the death in the newspaper. He said to David John, the licensee: 'What have you got to worry about? I was with a woman last night and she was burnt to death!'

He telephoned the police and waited for them to collect him in a car. He pleaded not guilty to a charge of murder, and throughout the trial believed himself to be guiltless. As far as he was concerned, it was a consequence of an unfortunate drunken brawl.

The jury considered their verdict for an hour and found Mclean not guilty of murder, but guilty of manslaughter. He was sentenced to five years' penal servitude. Mr Justice Cassels said that he showed 'callous disregard for the safety of the creature whose body you were making use of'.

He had previously been convicted of house-breaking in 1935, and assault in 1936. Ruth herself was well known to the police. She frequented public houses and had been convicted some years earlier. This was probably not for traffic offences. But this is irrelevant. As the judge said: 'However low the woman might have sunk, however sordid her mode of living, she was within the law and entitled to live.'

STRANGER DANGER

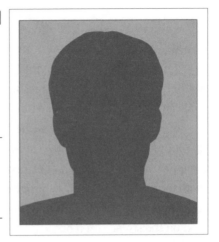

Suspect:	Thomas Williams
Age:	Forty-one
Charge:	Murder

It is every parent's nightmare: your child taken from you in broad daylight. The next time you see them, they are dead. This was the horror faced by the Macari family in the summer of 1941. To make matters worse, the police knew who did it. But they just couldn't make it stick.

The sculpture looks down on the Macari grave. (Author's collection)

Guistina Macari (known as Christina) was born in Antrim in Northern Ireland. Her father was Eugenio, a shopkeeper who had moved to Swansea to take over a fish and chip shop in Dillwyn Street. At the time of her murder, Guistina was three years old.

She was wearing a blue dress with a green jumper and white pinafore and she had dark brown bobbed hair. She was a confident, happy girl, who was well known to the bus conductors for her habit of hopping on and off the buses that used Dillwyn Street. She played in the shop, spoke to customers and was always friendly. On Saturday

17 May 1941 she had been playing outside. At 1 p.m. she had gone upstairs to see her mother, who was ill in bed. Her mother never saw her alive again.

Eileen Brennan, who worked in Macari's, was on her way to work and saw her walking up Mount Pleasant Hill with a strange man. Eileen raised the alarm. Other people saw them too and there is a direct progress in the sightings towards Fforestfach. They were seen on the streets, on a bus.

Her body was found on Sunday afternoon in a plantation at Fforestfach, on the road between Cadle and Caereithin. William Richards, thirteen, was searching amongst rhododendron bushes for empty bottles so he could redeem the deposit. It was a favourite place for courting couples. He found instead Guistina, lying fully clothed in an unnatural position. Her right shoe was missing, later to be recovered hanging from a branch, which seemed to suggest she had been killed elsewhere and then carried and dumped beneath the bushes. Her buttocks were exposed, her knickers torn and pulled down. There was blood seeping from her genitals. She had been sexually assaulted with fingers and then smothered. She had died at about 7 p.m., after being given chocolate and ice cream.

The police appealed for witnesses from the pulpit in chapels and churches and in cinemas. Scotland Yard was called in. A number of men were suspected, but police attentions came to focus on

SWANSEA DEATH MYSTERY

(Continued from Page One).

She had been playing near her home during the morning, and she went upstairs to see her mother, who was not well.

A little later she was missed, and, a search of the locality having been made, her distracted parents reported her absence to the police.

INFORMATION WANTED.

The police are now satisfied from their enquiries that the child was in the Mount Pleasant district a little while after being seen at her home. A man is said to have been near her, if not actually with her. Her movements after this are wrapped in mystery.

The child's photograph is reproduced again to-day at the request of

The Child.

the police, who are hoping that assistance will be forthcoming from some members of the public, who will recall having seen the small girl on Saturday afternoon or evening.

STURDY BUILD.

As already announced in the "Evening Post," Ginstina was wearing a blue dress, green jumper and white pinafore.

She is described as being Italian in appearance, with a full face, brown eyes, dark bobbed hair, and sturdy in build.

Acting Detective Inspector E. Jones, of the Swansea C.I.D., would welcome any information, however small, that would assist the police in tracing the child's movements.

Yesterday's post-mortem examination was conducted by Dr. Webster, the Home Office expert, in the presence of Dr. Harrison, of the Forensic Department of Cardiff City Police, and Dr. Vyvyan Davies, the Swansea police surgeon.

(By kind permission of SWW Media)

forty-one-year-old Thomas Williams of 20 Nicholl Street, about 50 yards from Dillwyn Street.

In the days following the murder, he was seen by neighbours washing his blue suit and drying it on the line, along with his mackintosh and his trilby. When he saw others looking at the clothes he hastily took them in. He also had his hair cut.

He was first called in for questioning on 31 May 1941. He had tried to escape through the back of the house and over a wall, but was found in an alley.

He was a man with an explosive temper. After one interview in Swansea Central in June, he had gone to see the doctor, Hayden Peters, to ask him to attend to his wife, who was upset because he had been picked up in connection with the murder. When Dr Peters refused,

(By kind permission of SWW Media)

saying it wasn't a case for the doctors, he became extremely agitated, shouting, 'I'll have you reported!'

On 27 June he was collected in a police car to attend an identity parade at Swansea Prison. He had to be restrained in the car. At the parade he was positively identified by Sarah Evans as the man she had seen on St Helens Road with a little girl at 1 p.m. Hers was compelling evidence. She had seen him leading the child away. Guistina had sweets in her hand. Alfred Berry also was certain he had seen Williams at 1.05 p.m. with a child in Mount Pleasant. He indicated Williams by touching him on the shoulder as required. Williams tried to strike him and had to be restrained.

'This is a f****** fix frame up by the police! Those f****** from Scotland Yard are behind this!'

Rees Jones identified him as the man he had seen on a seat in Mount Pleasant with a girl matching Guistina's description. Again, Williams tried to attack him: 'I'll bash you, you bastard! My brother-in-law will get you.'

Ernest Mugford indicated that he had seen him at a bus stop with a child at 3.30 p.m. Again Williams struck out, making contact this time. But significantly, four other witnesses couldn't identify him. One thought they had seen

'Those f****** from Scotland Yard are behind this!'

him buying chocolate macaroons; another at Mynydd Newydd at 9.30 p.m., a short distance from where the body was discovered. But they weren't sure.

Williams was taken back to Swansea Central, still in a rage. In the Chief Inspector's office he tore up papers relating to another case. When he was given tea, he threw it all over statements of evidence and smashed the mug. He was shouting and swearing. He attacked Detective Sergeant Tunsill by hitting him on top of the head with his fist. Thomas was bundled off to a cell to calm down. When he was taken to the charge room, he became tempestuous again.

He had an alibi which was corroborated to some extent by his wife Eva, although their stories didn't always match. Eva had a cleft palate and was hard to understand. The police said she was 'of low grade, mentally'.

She had gone to work on Saturday morning, cleaning for Dr Ritchings. Williams had gone shopping, buying potatoes, a piece of beef, cabbage and some sweets. In the afternoon he had listened to a football match on the radio. Then they had gone out to look at adverts in shop windows, since they were looking for new rooms. They had enjoyed a bedtime sweet and then retired to bed – to sleep. He said, 'I am incapable of having intercourse. My wife is forty-six years of age and she is not sexually inclined. I have never had intercourse with her.'

Shopkeepers didn't remember him. All they did remember was him turning up a few days later, to suggest that he had been there on that Saturday.

He said he'd never been to Fforestfach, but was recognised as a man who had asked for a jug of tea a few weeks earlier from a cottage only 50 yards from where Guistina was found. One witness identified him. The other did not. This was the pattern in all attempts to identify him. Whilst his long nose and slight frame made him stand out to some, others were less confident.

It was the unreliability of the identification that undermined the prosecution case when it reached court in Carmarthen in November 1941. If they couldn't make the identification stick, then the judge, Justice Lawrence, felt there was no need to proceed and Williams was discharged.

The Macari family grave in Danygraig Cemetery. (Author's collection)

The police described him as a 'criminal of many parts'. He had a teenage conviction for an indecent assault on a girl in Monmouth, for which he had been imprisoned for six weeks. In 1913 he had assaulted Annie Jones and exposed himself to another woman. He had also assaulted an eight-year old called Nellie Gould, who was picking blackberries in Pontypool. He pulled her behind bushes and tore her knickers to shreds, 'scratching her private parts'.

Guistina was eventually reunited with her mum and dad. They are buried together in Danygraig Cemetery together with her sister Orlandina, beneath an ornate and poignant memorial.

The police knew that Williams had done it. There was evidence that was never presented in court. There was hair on his coat that was microscopically identical with that of Guistina. Fibres found on his coat matched those on her frock. He would have walked across a recently manured field – and traces of pig and cow dung were found on his shoe. Yes, they had him, and yes, he got away – and the Macaris never tasted justice.

THE GUN WITH THE PERSPEX HANDLE

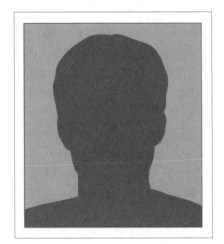

Suspect:	Unknown
Age:	Unknown
Charge:	None

The gun that shot her was found in the police museum in Bridgend. Muriel's blue coat, along with her underwear and school uniform, had been wrapped in a paper bag and stuffed away in a cupboard in Cockett Police Station when detectives believed their inquiries had reached a dead end.

But for some people this is a murder that won't go away. Even though it was over sixty years ago, the need for justice still burns strong. These items, together with recent forensic advances, have provided a real and unexpected opportunity.

Investigators have been able to extract enough fragments of DNA from a semen stain on the back of Muriel's coat to revive hope that the identity of her killer could be revealed in one of the world's oldest 'cold case' investigations. Now they have a DNA profile of her killer. It does not match any profile currently in the records, but there is always the hope that they can one day use it to identify the family from which the killer came.

Contrast such careful research with the horror and mayhem of Muriel's final moments.

Muriel Joan Drinkwater was a clever girl. She wanted to be a teacher. She was lively, inquisitive and happy. It was just a few weeks before her thirteenth birthday. She returned to her home at Tyle-Du Farm on the bus from Gowerton Girls Intermediate School on 27 June 1946. Today the area has been lost beneath the motorway services at Penllergaer and the new housing estate behind. In those days it was much more remote, and Muriel had to walk through the forest to get home. It was a lonely walk, but it was a route she and her sisters had taken a thousand times. They would cross the Melin Llan Bridge and the Pontlliw to Llangyfelach railway line, then go up the hill to the farmhouse.

It was 4.30 p.m. and Muriel's mother Margaret was making a pot of tea when she looked from the window down the hill and saw her daughter about 400 yards away.

She walked into the yard outside the farmhouse and they waved to each other. A dip in the track then took Muriel out of sight into an area of dense fir and spruce. Margaret returned to the kitchen and filled the teapot with hot water.

Muriel never arrived home.

In that dip in the track she was raped and then shot in the chest, left lying in the undergrowth, just a few minutes away from home. *The South Wales Evening Post* told readers that at this spot there 'were patches of fern and brambles in which a man may sink out of sight. No writer of detective fiction could devise a more suitable setting for a crime story'.

The image reported in the paper of her singing and swinging her satchel as she went home innocently along an isolated woodland path where a man was lying in wait for her, still has the power to chill.

Having seen her daughter so close to home, Margaret thought Muriel must be playing somewhere. But all through that night her father, Percy, searched the woods with dozens of village men and police, vainly calling out her name in the torrential rain.

Muriel was found the following morning. She had been brutally beaten around the head and then shot twice in the chest at point-blank range. The killer had thrown the gun into nearby undergrowth.

A police spokesman said: 'The child was foully murdered in a terrible way. She was twice shot in the breast and her head was bashed in. She was badly mauled as well.'

The murder weapon was a Colt .45 American army pistol, manufactured in the Springfield Armoury in 1942 and then sent out to Europe.

(By kind permission of SWW Media)

Significantly it had one distinctive feature. The original wooden handle had been adapted with the addition of a perspex grip.

During the war many American servicemen were stationed at Penllergaer and it was thought that one of them may have sold the gun to someone else. As a result, suspicions were tightly and perhaps cruelly focused.

They hoped the perspex would provide vital leads. After all, a similar weapon had been used in the murder of a cinema manager in Bristol.

But their enquiries came to nothing. There were no witnesses. No real leads. Men were questioned across the whole of South Wales but nothing emerged and eventually the trail went cold. Her clothes were packed away and forgotten about, leaving the people of Penllergaer looking at each other in fear and suspicion.

(By kind permission of SWW Media)

The Drinkwater family has long gone. Muriel's parents and sisters are all dead. The farm has disappeared, remembered only in the name of a housing development.

Three thousand people attended her funeral. In 2007 the local Girl Guide troop, of which Muriel had once been a member, paid for a new headstone to replace the simple cross on her grave at St David's Church in Penllergaer, remembering an ordinary girl lost and now consigned to history.

There have always been theories and accusations. A strange, smartly dressed man had been seen lurking in the woods. The murder was linked to other, viciously disturbing, murders of young girls in Abertillery. Then it was connected to the murder of Sheila Martin, aged eleven in Kent. That murder too remains unsolved. But until recently there has been no hope of real progress.

Suspicion has lived in the village ever since that day, and the older generation still waits for closure. As they said at the time, 'None of us will be free men again until this murderer is caught.' Was it really possible that perhaps the person who did it was someone they knew?

Muriel is the girl who never grew up. She has never moved on from that open, innocent face that has stared out from the newspapers for over sixty years. We will never be able to know what she might have become. She was cheated and robbed of her future. All she has now is notoriety.

(Author's collection)

The murder has a fatal fascination for some, who remain convinced that they can solve the crime. Amateurs crawl over the case to such an extent that the official files are now closed to the public and have been made exempt from Freedom of Information requests. The need to be the first to name names burns brightly in some and does not assist official enquiries.

The place where she died is not a nice place. Don't go there. It is a place where grim-looking men wait in cars for casual encounters. Beyond their lair, the path where she died still has a disturbing power. There is something unsettling. A memory of screams and pain embedded in the landscape. It is not a place where a child should die, so close to home, so suddenly and so cruelly. It is not a place for anyone.

FINALLY ...

Much has been said of the drunkenness and immorality of our town, and not without cause; for no observant person can fail to be impressed by the sad pictures of our principal streets, so thickly set with all grades of public house and so frequently teeming with a debauched, besotted crowd. A Saturday evening's walk through High Street, and many other thoroughfares, will induce painful thoughts of our common human-ity, and will raise the blush at the expense of our boasted Christian and philanthropic efforts. These scenes we have always before our eyes, and to a great extent familiarity hides their hideousness, but ever and anon some harrowing detail of a life of crime, or some dire result of a drunken frolic, comes to the surface, and as, in the light of this revelation, we gaze on the abominations that surround us, we awake to their terrible significance.

The *Cambrian* newspaper, 2 January 1874

If you enjoyed this book, you may also be interested in…

Bloody Welsh History: Swansea

GEOFF BROOKES

Swansea has a long and dangerous past. Viking raids, English attacks, factory riots, deadly diseases…all have left their mark on the city, some of which can still be seen today. Geoff Brookes' fascinating insight into Swansea's gruesome history looks at every brutal happening between AD 43 and 1947, including the Battle of Llwchr and the Rebecca Riots. With over seventy illustrations and photographs, this book is an enthralling glimpse into a dark past.

9780752480534

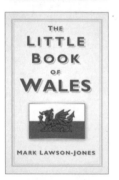

Denbighshire Folk Tales

FIONA COLLINS

Denbighshire is the oldest inhabited area of Wales. Its varied landscape has inspired many tales of ancient battles, strange creatures and curious customs. Dragons and devils, witches, cunning men, and the Fair Folk loom large in the county's history. From epic tales of magic and mystery to ordinary people doing extraordinary things Fiona Collins has collected all of these stories and retells them here, alongside illustrations from local artist Ed Fisher.

9780752451879

The Little Book of Wales

MARK LAWSON JONES

This little book is an intriguing compendium of everything Welsh. Everything from eccentric inhabitants, traditional food and sports is covered here, from the historical to the plain bizarre. Packed with facts and light-hearted details, the Little Book of Wales is a volume that can be dipped into over and over again – a never-ending source of fascinating and quirky facts. This is essential reading for visitors and locals alike.

9780752489278

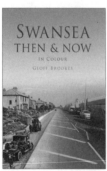

Swansea Then & Now

GEOFF BROOKES

Swansea has a rich, absorbing past, which is reflected in this delightful full-colour compilation. Contrasting a selection of forty-five archive images alongside modern photographs taken from the same location. Beneath the sad anonymity of a post-war city, devastated by the Blitz, the vestiges of something more distinguished still remain. This volume provides a fascinating and nostalgic look at Swansea as it used to be.

9780752465258

Visit our website and discover thousands of other History Press books.

www.thehistorypress.co.uk